Top 10
Bible Doctrines

Dr. J. Ronald Nyberg, Jr.
(A.A., A.S., B.S., M.A., Ph.D.)

Cover designs provided by Natalie Grace Nyberg.

ISBN 978-1-940356-00-6

Preface

There is a spiritual drought and famine in the land. The majority do not know God or His Word; therefore, many are confused about basics questions, such as, "From where did I come? Where am I going? What is my purpose?" The Bible is the most influential Book ever written, and it is part of the Great Books Curriculum. Though many own a copy of the Bible, most have never completely read the Bible through, even once. Most are unaware of the most important topics in the universe—eternal truth, much less the top ten basic Bible doctrines. Many cannot even summarize the top Ten Commandments, out of the 613 listed. Even strong churches are weak in their attempts to teach the top Bible doctrines in a systematic way. Many churches dilute their teachings to such a degree that they don't teach what the Bible says, skip the politically incorrect topics, or only teach the "feel good" messages that people want to hear. Our thirty second sound bite society makes this task even more challenging for young Christians to ever hear God's basic truths. Parishioners are often unwilling, or sometimes even unable to study the lengthy multivolume or scholarly doctrinal sets. Thus, it is no wonder that modern day Christians are prime targets for the empty, clever, and deceptive worldly philosophies and false religions of the many emerging cult groups.

Due to its importance, most suppose that there is a great number of sound Bible doctrine books already published. Having been a theology professor and Bible teacher for many years, it shocked me to learn there wasn't much available to aid in this process of educating the student who hungers to know the truths of God's Word. I discovered very scholarly 10-30 volume sets and deep individual books on a single doctrine, which were commonly difficult to follow. I observed high-level reviews missing many key teachings. Some of the works which I reviewed failed to stress topics of great importance across many doctrines. Generally, most mentioned theological terms or quoted other works, but few had scriptures to clearly make it "Bible Doctrines." Oftentimes, the passages referenced had related words, but were not contextually related to the teaching it claimed to be supporting. In teaching just the Top

i

Ten Bible Doctrines for over three decades, it has been a joy to observe students that hungered, were amazed and thrilled at the basics of our great faith. The simplicity and clarity of God's Word on these deep, important, and eternal topics is enthralling. I pray that you will find this book a key learning tool and resource in your library. As you study these pages, it is my prayer that you open God's Word and read for yourself the Scripture that will come alive in your heart. It will surely accomplish what God intends in your life as you seek to know Him through His Word.

Although more difficult to read, I intentionally have listed the references in the text, maintaining that this is a reference book with the Scripture as the primary authority for each point, certainly above what this author, or others may state. Bible references are also bolded for emphasis and ease in locating. I also intentionally chose not to cite many other authors, but have significantly quoted the Scripture passages themselves, or cited numerous Bible references (which, ironically, few Bible Doctrines books do).

Brief Description (<u>What are the major ten Bible doctrines?</u>)
This book is a scriptural and systematic study of the fundamental tenets of the ten major Bible doctrines including the study of: the Bible, God the Father, Jesus Christ, the Holy Spirit, man, sin, salvation, angels, the church, and final events.

Purpose (<u>What are the goals of this book?</u>)
My intent in this book is first to glorify God. I pray that this compilation will readily provide this resource at minimal cost, to as many as possible. I also pray that this work will educate and lead the unsaved to the truth, and equip, mature, and protect the saved. Additionally, I pray that a systematic study of these truths will stimulate deep thought and love for the depth and riches of God and His Word. This reference may also provide a basic tailorable curriculum for those who teach in Churches, Christian schools, colleges, universities, and seminaries. More advanced outcomes include the ability to understand and discuss the critical sub doctrines of each major doctrine while defending their faith in dialogue with others. I consider this work a bedside companion, a

complete desk reference, a coffee table guidebook, and a comprehensive manual that covers the basic truths that span the entire Bible. It is my hope that this will be a valuable tool for any life-long learner and follower of Jesus Christ.

<u>Why Unique</u> (<u>Why different from other Bible doctrine books?</u>)

- Top ten key Bible doctrines (not a 100; averages < 10 pages each in an 8 ½ x 11 format)
- Concise and thorough coverage of each doctrine (doesn't cherry pick or skip due to difficulty)
- Numerous Scripture quotes (over 250) and references (about 4,000) and not lots of fluff or undefined scholarly words
- Briefly outlines each doctrine (systematically organized)
- Protects against the proselytizing of cults and error of political correctness by being informed and educated

<u>Order</u>

Many Bible Doctrine books begin with God because He truly is before and the author of all; One must believe that He first exists, before believing that He has spoken to us through the unique, inspired Book called the Holy Scriptures. Also, many false religions and cults claim to believe in God, yet emphasize and rely upon extra Biblical literature as their authority, above Scripture itself. Some define God differently than the God of the Bible. Finally, since this is "Bible" Doctrines or teachings, I have chosen to begin with the Bible first, as it is the Source and greatest authority on God and each of the other important doctrines. If one doesn't come to trust and understand first how God has best revealed each of these teachings through the trustworthy unique Book called the Holy Bible, all other teachings are of no consequence.

As the reader you may choose any order for this study, but I have listed the doctrines in what I believe is the most sequential and logical order. I battled hard to not make each of these doctrines into a lengthy book so that each could be studied within a short or lengthy individual class session. May God open your heart and mind as He reveals more of His Word on these life changing topics!

Acknowledgements

I first must thank my God, my Lord and Savior Jesus Christ for saving me, giving me purpose, giving me a home in heaven, giving me hope in a dark and dying world, and giving such wisdom through such a special revelation and guide for everything in His Holy Bible. God's Spirit, working through His Word, has changed me more than anyone and everyone else combined.

Certainly I want to thank my Godly parents for loving me, teaching me, requiring me to memorize large portions of God's Word, providing me many expensive educational opportunities in many years of Christian schools. My Dad faithfully showed me his heart and passion for the lost and less fortunate, bringing many outcasts into our home and staying up all night sharing with them the gospel and teachings of our Lord Jesus Christ. I have seen him hire many folks off the street and pay them to hear God's way and see many have their lives turned around completely as they were saved and saw my Dad as their spiritual Dad. My wonderful Mom faithfully studied God's Word, loved, cherished, and happily served My Dad, my siblings, and me. She is an example that prompts all who know her to wish they had her in their life. Her daily prayers, encouraging, and requests to listen to what God was doing in my life shaped me greatly at key times.

I want to thank my brother, Dr. Jon Jeffrey Nyberg for his faithful leadership, ministry, encouragement, and friendship. He truly is a friend who sticks closer than even a brother. I truly believe in him and his Church Planting ministries to lead many to Christ, build them up in the truth, and dream to plant a 1,000 churches in his lifetime. See www.steppingstonesministry.org for a very worthwhile spiritual investment or just to pray for this great man and work of God.

Thank you to numerous friends, pastors, teachers, co-workers, and students who have faithfully shared their time, wisdom, and passion for God and His Word over countless years. Special moments included a forgotten pastor / teacher who told me to "read a chapter of Proverbs a day (31 chapters) will make you the wisest person around". Thanks to Dr. Irving L. Jensen for sharing his inductive Bible study methods including charting Bible passages, chapters, and Books. Thanks to Dallas Theological Seminary for their emphasis on a literal hermeneutics leading to Biblical clarity and permitting the main point of a passage and its supporting arguments best be understood and communicated to others. Thanks to my sister Beth who strongly encouraged me to stop everything and get this work published and my sister Kim for her prayers.

A special thanks to my wonderful wife (Gay Nyberg), mother and primary teacher of my three great children (Natalie, James, and Noah). What a blessing and faithful companion. She has encouraged me with her passion for God and His Word and her tremendous teaching abilities God has given her. She has humbled me as she has quoted chapters of God's Word from memory and wanted to discuss deep spiritual insights. She frequently reads through the entire Bible several times each year. I also want to thank her for the final editing of this work. She encouraged me on this book saying "if no one else receives the blessing that we get every time we read this, it is clearly a legacy for us and our children."

And finally, thanks to you as you read this. May God bless you and keep you as He desires to do forever . . .

Table of Contents

The greatest written revelation of His-story, authoritative for faith, eternal life, and happiness—the Bible is the most popular, published, translated, studied, most accurate ancient literature, and influential Book ever! This must be God's Book to man!

Introduction

Bibliology comes from the Greek word *"biblos"*, meaning book, and *"logos"*, meaning a word about, the science of, or the study of; thus **Bibliology is the study of the Book, the Bible, or the Scriptures.** Some Key Verses are **2Ti. 2:15; 3:14-17; 2Pe. 1:19-21; Heb. 4:12; Rev. 22:18-19; Mat. 4:4; Psa. 119:9, 11, 105, 130; 138:2, 4. 2Ti. 2:15** says, "Study to shew thyself approved unto God, a workman that needeth not to be ashamed, rightly dividing the word of truth." **2Ti. 3:14-17**—"But continue in the things which you have learned and have been assured of, knowing of whom you have learned them; And that from a child you have known The Holy Scriptures, which are able to make you wise unto salvation through faith which is in Christ Jesus. All scripture *is* given by inspiration of God, and *is* profitable for doctrine, for reproof, for correction, for instruction in righteousness, that the man of God may be perfect, thoroughly furnished unto all good works." **2Pe. 1:19-21**—"We have also a more sure word of prophecy; whereunto ye do well that ye take heed, as unto a light that shineth in a dark place, until the day dawn, and the day star arise in your hearts. Knowing this first, that no prophecy of the scripture is of any private interpretation. For the prophecy came not in old time by the will of man, but holy men of God spoke *as they were* moved by the Holy Ghost." **Heb. 4:12**—"For the word of God is quick, and powerful, and sharper than any two-edged sword, piercing even to the dividing asunder of soul and spirit, and of the joints and marrow, and is a discerner of the thoughts and intents of the heart." **Rev. 22:18-19**—"For I testify unto every man that heareth the words of the prophecy of this book, If any man shall add unto these things, God shall add unto him the plagues that are written in this book: And if any man shall take away from the words of the book of this prophecy, God shall take away his part out of the book of life, and out of the holy city, and from the things which are written in this book." **Mat. 4:4**—"But he answered and said, It is written, Man shall not live by bread alone, but by every word that proceedeth out of the mouth of God." **Psa. 119:9, 11**—"How shall a young man cleanse his way? By taking heed thereto according to Your Word. Your Word have I hid in my heart, that I might not sin against You." **Psa. 119:105**—"Your Word is a lamp unto my feet, and a light unto my path." **Psa. 119:130**—"The entrance of Your Words gives light; it gives understanding unto the simple." **Psa. 138:2, 4**—"I will worship toward Your holy temple, and praise Your name for Your loving-kindness and for Your truth: for You have magnified Your word above all Your name. All the kings of the earth shall praise You, O LORD, when they hear the words of Your mouth."

How Would God Communicate to Man?

1. <u>Spoken</u> word for intimacy.
2. <u>Written</u> to last for many.
3. <u>Progressively</u> to build upon the previous, for different groups, at key times, through key individuals.
4. <u>Compare to things known</u> so that man would understand.
5. <u>Common language</u> for common man, not just the intellectuals.
6. <u>Miraculously confirmed</u> to prove it was from God.
7. <u>Containing major themes</u> (the Bible, God, Jesus, Spirit, man, sin, salvation, church, angels, and final things).
8. <u>Through yourself in human flesh</u> in the Person of Jesus Christ, Who is God's Word and spoke in His Word.

That is exactly what God did in His Holy Bible!

7 Steps of God's Word to Man (Progressive Revelation)

Revelation: Receiving the Truth

Inspiration: Recording the Truth

Transmission: Rewriting the Truth

Canonization: Recognizing the Truth

Preservation: Protecting the Truth

Translation: Propagating the Truth

Illumination: Perceiving the Truth

1—Revelation: Receiving the Truth (This was finished when Scripture was completed in the first century AD after the final book of the bible, Revelation, was complete). This was progressively and specially revealed as each Book in the Bible was completed and is closely coupled with the inspiration of the Scriptures.

2—Inspiration: Recording the Truth (This was finished when Scripture was complete). Greek word "Theos" - God, "Pneustos" - Breathed ("Theospneustos"—God Breathed). The Holy Spirit conveyed to and through man (using their individual personalities) the exact meaning and words of God. This was the Divine condescension of God to man (from the Infinite to the finite, somewhat illustrated in the enormity of explaining of astrophysics to a child). Seven major views of the Scripture are as follows: (1) Modernistic as written by man, though not inspired by God at all, (2) Naturalistic as from God, but like any other "inspirational" book, similarly being inspired by love, (3) Neo-Orthodox (Carl Barth) view in which it becomes true as understood by reader, though not true by itself, (4) Partial inspiration as only in spiritual parts, not in scientific or historical aspects, (5) Concept—Concepts were inspired, not words. (6) Dictation or Mechanical-- Human Type writers. (7) Verbal, Plenary, or Full (**2Ti. 3:16-17; 2Pe. 1:19-21**). Divine truths were shaped in human molds. The men and the words were inspired (breathed into man, and out to the page). God superintended the recording. Inerrancy—Because of Inspiration, the Bible is without error. Infallibility—Because of Inspiration, The Bible has Divine authority (incapable of error or failing). Syllogism for Inerrancy and Infallibility (God cannot err or lie. The Bible is inspired by God. Therefore, The Bible cannot err or lie).

3—Transmission: Rewriting the Truth (This means the same language; it is ongoing as needed, desired, or required). This was performed by a special group of people called Scribes. These Scribes faithfully copied the original manuscripts like human copy machines, before there was even a typewriter or computer. This was an art and science. The Scribes took baths before copying, letter counting, dividing, and even burned their copies when deemed unreadable or with error. The Scribal profession was a calling where they prided themselves in their quality assurance to the greatest degree. The Dead Sea Scrolls provided strong confirmation of the Bible's reliability and how well these Scribes performed their sacred duty. Thousands of copies exist today. The same written words and language as the original autographs were confirmed by Dead Sea Scrolls. During 1947 to 1979, over 1,000 documents in Hebrew, Aramaic, and Greek that dated back to 200 BC were found. This confirmed word-for-word the Bible that we hold in our hands today. This amazing discovery, probably in the only place in the world (11 caves in Qumran in the northwest corner of Dead Sea shore) where the weather would permit these scrolls to survive and remain legible after over 2,000 years. These are now available to the public.

4—Canonization: Recognizing the Truth (The collection of Scripture has been completed). Canonicity refers to the Church councils observing the books which have been faithfully set apart and passed down from generation to generation, and recognizing what is and isn't God's true Word. Many different groups and councils have confirmed God's Holy Word. The Bible is Scripture because of Divine Authority, not man's attestation. Man did recognize and collected books when written to the Canon based on three criteria: (1) Prophets, Apostles, and Jesus claim as Scripture, and the inspired Word of God confirmed by miracles. (2) God's people (Israel and the Church) claim as Scripture. (3) Doctrine claims it as Scripture. It is consistent with other Scripture and known Scripture calls It Scripture. God said His Word was miraculously attested in His Word by miracles and prophecy; it was agreed upon as God's Word when added to the existing canon, and it was attested by both Jesus and Jews in the OT, and the Apostles and the Church, both in the OT and NT).

The Apocrypha (which later became accepted by some Roman Catholics and Eastern Orthodox churches) did not have the consensus of which books should be included. Current Catholic Bibles have added the Apocrypha, which many thought reactionary to the authority of Scripture and Martin Luther's Protestant Reformation. The Apocrypha is the most accepted of all pseudepigrapha, or false writings (2Th. 2:2). Many have asked why the 1611 KJV includes the Apocrypha. I believe this is because they are good historical references (not Scripture) during the 400 silent years between the Old and New Testaments, when God did not speak through His prophets. Almost all Bibles include other non - Biblical introductions, prefaces, maps, pictures, concordances, CROSS-references, titles, numbers (for chapters, verses, page numbers), commentaries, study notes, etc. The original 1611 KJV includes other historical items, such as a message from King James, a message from the translators with historical references to Queen Elizabeth, St. Jerome, St. Augustine, Origen, English Lords, Parliament, etc. Clearly, all these people referenced are not Scripture. Most Christians agree that there are three strikes against the Apocrypha in its content, lack of consensus, and claims). (1) Content alone - contradicts Scripture. It does not have Divine fingerprints or miraculous confirmation. It has superstitious magic. It has many errors. (2) Consensus Alone - NONE. It is not a part of the Jewish OT Canon. In fact, the Jews rejected it was when written and still do. It is never quoted or claimed to be Scripture by Jesus or Apostles. It is never quoted or claimed to be Scripture by the early Church. It is patently rejected by Protestants. Many notable Catholics have rejected the Apocrypha, including St. Jerome, and others given sainthood by the Roman Catholic Church. Only later in 1546 at Council of Trent did the Catholic church call the Apocrypha Scripture. (3) Internal claims. Most importantly, the Bible itself does not claim it to be Scripture. Striking is the juxtaposition of **1Co. 14:37-38** and **Gal. 1:8-9** with II Maccabees 15:38 stating ". . . if it is poorly done and mediocre, that was the best I could do."

5—Preservation: Protecting the Truth (ongoing). This is God's divine preservation from Satan's attacks to add or take away from His Word. **Mat. 5:18**–"For verily I say unto you, 'til heaven and earth pass, one jot or one tittle shall in no wise pass from the law, till all be fulfilled." A jot and tittle are the smallest Hebrew markings (e.g., a jot would be a straight line of an "i" and a tittle would be the dot above it). **Mat. 24:35**—"Heaven and earth shall pass away, but my Words shall not pass away." Many have tried to destroy Scripture. Here are a few historic examples: Emperor Diocletian (303 AD) ordered the destruction of all Bibles trying to eradicate Christianity.

Twenty-five years later Constantine declared Christianity an official religion and ordered printing 50 copies at the government's expense. Pope Innocent III (1199 AD) ordered the burning of all Bibles, but this made the Bible more cherished. Pope Clement VIII exhumed John Wycliffe's grave, burned his bones, and threw his ashes in a river, because of John Wycliffe's incredible and life-long translation efforts. The persecution of William Tyndale was to prevent people from getting copies of the Word of God in their hands. Voltaire died in 1728 and said that in 100 years there would be no more Bibles. Fifty years later, the Geneva Bible Society was producing Bibles from their printing presses in the former home of Voltaire. Statistics vary but are commonly thought that 80% of books are forgotten in one year. Only ½ of 1 (.5) % of books survive for seven years. About 4,000 years since the Pentateuch was written, and the Word of God still stands (although one of my science books has had 29 revisions to correct errors, my Bible has had none).

6—Translation: Propagating the Truth (Different languages, ongoing). Scholars of the original Hebrew, Aramaic, Greek, and other languages faithfully translate God's Word into other languages so that those who don't know the original languages could have God's Word in their own native tongue. Wycliffe Bible translators (http://www.wycliffe.org) have translated over 700 languages of the known 6,800 spoken languages in the world and have over 1,500 translations in progress. There are more Bibles translated and published in more languages than in any other book. In fact, there are many languages that have the Bible as their only written book. Over six billion Bibles have been published and distributed. The Gideons International provides free Bibles to over a million people around the world every week (http://www.gideons.org).

The OT (originally written in Hebrew and some Aramaic) was completed around 400 BC. One of the first and most important Bible translations of the OT was the **Septuagint** (LXX) in Greek in the third century BC providing an excellent translation into the new world empire and language of the people. The NT was completed (originally written in Koine Greek) around 95 AD. Some of the most complete and important translations of the Bible include the **Latin**

Vulgate (405 AD), which also was the new world Roman empire and language of the people; **John Wycliffe**'s handwritten English Bible (1382 AD); Erasmus' Greek/Latin NT (1516); Martin Luther's German Bible (1522); **William Tyndale**'s NT (1526); the **Geneva Bible** (1560 AD) *which first added chapters and verses for easier locating and referencing*, **King James Version**-KJV (1611), **American Standard**-ASV, RSV, ESV (1901), **Revised Standard** (1952/1971), **New American Standard** Bible-NASB, NASV, NAS (1971, 1995), The Living Bible-TLB (1971, *not a translation, but only a paraphrase*, the **New International Version** NIV (1978, 1984), **New King James Version**-NKJV (1982), **English Standard** (2001/2007), The Message-MSB (2002), *also not a translation, but only a paraphrase*, the **Holman Christian Standard Bible**-HCSB (2004), the New Living Translation-NLB (1996, 2004), etc.

Some of the most accurate English translations today include the NKJV, KJV, NASB, and NIV. Translations are needed as often as there are new languages or changes in words, grammar, or syntax meaning or rules. Many words change meaning, especially over time. Many believe the KJV is the only true Bible, or the only Word of God. The KJV was not even translated until 1611; therefore, the nation of Israel, Jesus, the Apostles, and the entire Church did not even have the KJV until after 1611. Of course, not all speak English today, though English is commonly thought to be the universal language. The KJV is a great and lasting translation. There is one Bible, but many translations or versions, and even paraphrases. A paraphrase is not "God's Word," but is man putting God's Word into their own words. The question is debated, "Which translation is best?"

Literal ←NKJV-KJV-NAS-ESV-NIV-HCS-NLB-MSG-TLB→ **Loose**

Three ways describe translation precision or equivalence of meaning.
1. <u>Formal</u>—Complete ("Literal" or "word-for -word").
2. <u>Functional</u>—Meaning/Concept ("Dynamic" or "thought-for-thought").
3. <u>Failing</u>—Some ("Intent" or "food-for-thought").

Whole volumes are written on Textual Criticism and limited time and space prevent the Textual or Higher Criticism issues in this book. Noteworthy is that the NKJV/KJV uses the Textus Receptus, Received Text, or the Majority Text, where other translations have gone to the more modern Alexandrian including Codex Sinaiticus and Codex Vaticanus) These are small differences, but a handful of excluded words, phrases, and paragraph.

Attempts to provide "ease of reading" or "clarity" blur Translation or "Propagating the Truth" with Illumination or "Perceiving the Truth". It almost moves from (Observation→ Interpretation→ Application) as you step thru the arrow continuum. Also, the farther to the right on the arrow, the less notes are provided of the "license" (looseness) translators took regarding the what, and when, and why they made certain choices in their translations.

7—Illumination: Perceiving the Truth (ongoing). The Holy Spirit enlightens the minds of people to God's truth, especially from His Word. Enlightenment removes spiritual blindness and leads to salvation (**2Co. 4:2-6; 2Ti. 3:15**). Enlightenment intensifies and truly begins at salvation (**Pro. 1:7; 9:10; 1Co. 2:10-15**). Enlightenment continues as we hear and apply God's Word (**Psa. 19:8; Eph. 1:18**). ALL Truth is God's Truth, not just the Bible. God can and does use ALL truth (and sources of truth) to enlighten the minds of the saved and unsaved.

Biblical Names

Etymology: Derived from the Greek word "Biblos" meaning Book. Since the word "Bible" is not found in the Holy Bible, this is where the name Bible came from and why it was used for the Holy Bible. Ancient Books written on "papyrus", led to paper (scrolls and then later book form codices), some on parchment or higher quality vellum (animal skins) and others with wood, stone, clay, or wax tablets. "Biblos" became applied to the sacred Books of the Bible ("Byblos" was Greek for papyrus and believed to be derived from the Phoenician city, Byblos. Since Scripture was the primary Book of Books written, it became applied to Scripture as the Bible), not just book, or a book, but The Book, The Holy Bible.

Below are Biblical names or words the Bible uses to refer to itself. "Scripture(s)": Sacred or Holy Writings (**Mat. 22:29; Mar. 12:10, 24; 15:28; Luk. 4:21; 24:27; Joh. 2:22; 5:39; 7:38; 10:35; Act 17:11; Rom. 1:22; 4:3; Gal. 4:30; 2Ti. 3:15; 2Pe. 1:20; 3:16**). "The Word of God": Revelation from God (**Mar. 7:13; Rom. 10:17; 2Cor. 2:17; Heb. 4:12; 1Th. 2:13**). "Your Word", "Law", "Commandments", "Testimonies", "Precepts", "Statutes", "Judgments" (**Psa.119**). "The Revelation of Jesus Christ" (**Gal. 1:12; 1Pe. 1:13; Rev. 1:1**).

Biblical Languages

The original manuscripts were written and subsequently copied for the OT (Old Testament or Old Covenant) primarily in Hebrew, except Aramaic in **Dan. 2:4-7:28; Ezr. 4:8-6:18; 7:12-26**. The NT (New Testament or New Covenant) was written in Koine Greek, the common language of the people. Koine Greek is somewhat different than Modern Greek that is spoken in Greece today and the classical Greek or scholarly Greek written by Socrates, Plato, Aristotle, etc.

Biblical Divisions

The Old Testament consists of 39 Books (Genesis to Malachi) with three major divisions. The Historical division includes 17 Books (Genesis—Esther), subdivided into the five Pre-Canaan Books (Genesis—Deuteronomy, called Torah, Pentateuch, or Law), the 12 Canaan Books (Joshua—2 Chronicles), and three Post-Exilic Books (Ezra, Nehemiah, and Esther). Exilic denotes Israel's exile into captivity. The second main division is consists of five Poetical or Wisdom Books (Job to Song of Solomon). The third major division consists of 17 Prophetical Books (Isaiah to Malachi). It is subdivided into five Major Books (Isaiah to Daniel). It is further subdivided into two categories, one with two Pre-exilic Books (Isaiah and Jeremiah) and one with three Exilic Books (Lamentations, Ezekiel, and Daniel). The final subdivision of the Prophetic Books consists of 12 Minor Books (Hosea to Malachi). These Minor Books have three subdivisions: eight Pre-Exilic Books (Hosea to Zephaniah), one Exilic Book (Obadiah), and three Post-Exilic Books (Haggai, Zechariah, and Malachi). Major are called major due to their length or size, and Minor are called so because of their brevity in length. These designations are not inspired, not due to better prophecies, or "more inspired"; a Book was either inspired by God or not, there is never a degree of inspiration.

The New Testament consists of 27 Books (Matthew to Revelation), also with three major divisions. The <u>Historical</u> division includes five Books (Matthew to Acts). The second main division consists of 21 Doctrinal or Epistolary, in the form of a letter, Books (Romans to Jude). It is subdivided into 13 or 14 Pauline Books (Romans to Philemon; named after Its recipients or human author; Hebrews was written to the Hebrew Christians). It is further subdivided into two categories, one with nine Impersonal or General Books (Romans to 2 Thessalonians) and one with four Personal or Pastoral Books (1 Timothy—Philemon). The Doctrinal or Epistolary final subdivision includes seven or eight Non-Pauline Books (James to Jude; named after the author, noting perhaps the exception of the Book of Hebrews). The third and final division is only one Prophetical Book (Revelation). Epistolary or Epistle just means letter. Although some joke that an Epistle is the wife of an Apostle.

<u>Authorship (Number and Names)</u>
There were about 34 to 42 total human co-authors of the Bible. The Old Testament (OT) had about 26 to 33 co-authors with seven unknown. Listed below are the **Author**, Book <u>name</u>, and Psalms (specific <u>chapters</u> with several different co-authors)

The OT's first stated co-author and Book was **Moses**—<u>Genesis</u>, <u>Exodus</u>, <u>Leviticus</u>, <u>Numbers</u>, <u>Deuteronomy</u>, <u>Psalms 90</u>. Then **Joshua**—<u>Joshua</u>, **Samuel**—<u>1 and 2 Samuel</u>, **Ezra**—<u>Ezra</u>, **Nehemiah**—<u>Nehemiah</u>, **David**—<u>Psalms</u> (73 of them designated Psalms of David), **Asaph**—<u>Psalms 50, 73-83</u>, **Heman** (the Ezrahite)—<u>Psalms 88</u>, **Ethan** (the Ezrahite)—<u>Psalms 89</u>, **Solomon**—<u>Psalms 72, 127</u>; <u>Proverbs</u>, <u>Ecclesiastes</u>, and <u>Song of Solomon</u>, **Isaiah**—<u>Isaiah</u>, **Jeremiah**—<u>Jeremiah</u> and <u>Lamentations</u>, **Ezekiel**—<u>Ezekiel</u>, **Daniel**—<u>Daniel</u>, **Hosea**—<u>Hosea</u>, **Joel**—<u>Joel</u>, **Amos**—<u>Amos</u>, **Obadiah**—<u>Obadiah</u>, **Jonah**—<u>Jonah</u>, **Micah**—<u>Micah</u>, **Nahum** (the Elkoshite)—<u>Nahum</u>, **Habakkuk**—<u>Habakkuk</u>, **Zephaniah**—<u>Zephaniah</u>, **Haggai**—<u>Haggai</u>, **Zechariah**—<u>Zechariah</u>, and **Malachi**—<u>Malachi</u>. Seven are **Unknown** or at least not stated in the Bible—Judges, Ruth (Talmud says Samuel), 1 and 2 Kings (many suggest Ezra, Ezekiel, or Jeremiah), 1 and 2 Chronicles (many believe Ezra), Esther (many suggest Ezra or Nehemiah), Job (many suggest Job, Elihu, Moses, Solomon, Hezekiah, Isaiah, or Ezra).

The New Testament (NT) had about eight to nine co-authors with seven unknown. The first co-author and Book was **Matthew**— Matthew, then **Mark**—Mark, **Luke**—Luke, Acts, **John**—John, 1, 2, 3 John, and Revelation, **Paul**—Romans, 1 and 2 Corinthians, Galatians, Ephesians, Philippians, Colossians, 1 and 2 Thessalonians, 1 and 2 Timothy, Titus, Philemon, **James**—James, **Peter**—1 and 2 Peter, and **Jude**—Jude. Only one is **unknown**—Hebrews. Many believe it was written by Paul because of the style, Greek usage, quotes, etc. Since the Jews tried to kill Paul multiple times, it would make sense not to call out his co-authorship when writing to the Jews or Hebrews.

Books of the Bible were **named** primarily by content, co-author, or recipients. Those named for **content** include Genesis, Exodus, Leviticus, Numbers, Deuteronomy, Judges, 1 and 2 Kings, 1 and 2 Chronicles, Esther (an exception, since not written by Esther), Psalms, Proverbs, Ecclesiastes, Song of Solomon (shown twice, here for "Song"), Lamentations; Acts, Philemon, Revelation). Those named after **co-authors** include Joshua, Ruth, 1 and 2 Samuel, Ezra, Nehemiah, Job, Song of Solomon (shown twice, here for "of Solomon"), Jeremiah, Ezekiel, Daniel, Hosea, Joel, Amos, Obadiah, Jonah, Micah, Nahum, Habakkuk, Zephaniah, Haggai, Zechariah, Malachi; Matthew, Mark, Luke, John, James, 1 and 2 Peter, 1, 2, and 3 John, and Jude. Those named after the **recipient(s)** include Romans, 1 and 2 Corinthians, Galatians, Ephesians, Philippians, Colossians, 1 and 2 Thessalonians, 1 and 2 Timothy, Titus, and Hebrews. Asaph, Heman, and Ethan were Levitical Musicians (**1Co. 15:17, 19**). There are also various discussions about the authorship of Proverbs including Agur, King Lemuel, and a compilation of Hezekiah's men.

<u>Divine Authorship and Internal Evidence</u>

Biblical Statements: There is one and only one Divine author, as there is only one God. The proof of God's authorship is evident in the Scripture as seen in **Dt. 6:6-9, 17-18; Jos. 1:8; 8:32-35; 2Sa. 22:31; Psa. 1:22; 12:6; 19:7 - 11; 93:5; 119:9, 11, 18; 89-93, 97-100, 104-105, 130; Pro. 30:5-6; Isa. 55:10 -11; Jer. 15:16; 23:29; Dan. 10:21; Mat. 5:17-19; 22:29; 24:35; Mar. 13:31; Luk. 16:17; Joh. 2:22; 5:24; 10:35; Act 17:11; Rom. 10:17; 1Co. 2:13; Col. 3:16; 1Th. 2:13; 2Ti. 2:15; <u>3:15-17</u>; 1Pe. 1:23-25; 2Pe. <u>1:19-21</u>; 3:15-16; Rev. 1:2; 22:19**. "Thus saith the Lord," "the Word of the Lord came unto me saying," "And the Lord said," "And God said," are found more than 3,800 times. *Most "so called" sacred books revered by false religions or cults don't even claim to be written by God. In sharp and distinct contrast, the Bible clearly states it was written by God.*

Biblical Continuity (Unity): There are many diverse <u>human authors</u> (doctor, tax collector, farmers, shepherds, fishermen, politicians, kings, prophets, priests, Jews, Romans, and Greeks). There are many diverse <u>locations or regions</u> (Canaan, Egypt, Babylon, Jerusalem, Samaria, Rome, etc.). There are many <u>years or periods over which It was written</u> (approximately 1,500 to 1,600 years). There are many different <u>events that it describes</u> (from the creation of the universe to the destruction of earth). Yet, it has one central, connective theme in the flow of history, without a single contradiction, and with perfect unity. This could only be guaranteed and maintained if from one Divine Author, God Himself. *Compare only one biology book, written in the same area, by the same author with one only written a few years ago. The lack of unity and continuity would be quite evident.*

Comprehensive Subject Matter (Depth): No human book is as complete. It is inexhaustible (poetry, science, theology, other religions, ethics, morality, warfare, history, philosophy, supernatural, anthropology, psychology, zoology, economy, dinosaurs, the origin and culmination of the universe). *Every time the Bible is read there is something new to see and learn!*

Literary Greatness (Accuracy): The Bible has the most accurate and greatest number of most ancient manuscripts with copies existing closest to the original. Stunningly, there are 5,686 Greek copies existing today of the NT within 30 to 100 years, with approximately 19,000 in various languages, with almost 100% accuracy where enough manuscripts can be seen to be completely reliable. The Bible even had people living who had seen the originals and copies. Homer's Iliad is considered the second most reliable ancient manuscript, written about 900BC with the first copy about 500 years later with 643 copies, and only 95% accuracy. Consider the confidence and accuracy assumed for Plato (7 copies found 1,200 years after written) and Aristotle's writings (49 copies found 1,400 years after written) whereas the accuracy cannot even be rated. This Bible is even more amazing from such a diverse group of human authors: farmers, fishermen, shepherds, physicians, prophets, priests, kings, tax collectors, Jews, Romans, Greeks, with great passages regarding the Ten Commandments (**Exo. 20; Deu. 5**), poetry (**Psa. 23; Lam. 3**), unanswerable questions (**Job 38-39**), wise sayings (**Proverbs**), God's Word (**Psa. 119**), music (**Psalms**), love songs (**Song of Solomon**), the Sermon of the Mount (**Mat. 5-7**), the Golden Rule (**Mat. 7:12**), the best definition of love (**1Co. 13**), the most quoted and referenced passage in the world (**Joh. 3:16**)—all considered the finest examples of writing.

Divine Authorship and External Evidence

The proof from select **Fulfilled Prophecy** (1,000s)**:** "Egypt...will no more rule over the nations" (**Ezr. 20:14-15** around sixth century BC). Egypt had been a world dominator and was defeated. This prophecy has been demonstrated for over 2,500 years, with the attempts to dominate Israel in 1948, 1967, 1973, and even currently. Even though rogue nations were ten times Israel's size, they have always been unsuccessful in their efforts to rule national Israel.

God's Word predicted and told Abraham, the Father of the Jews, that the Jews would be slaves in Egypt for 400 years, and then be strongly delivered. This was predicted three generations before the Jews even went to Egypt (when Abraham's wife was barren). Sarah gave birth to Isaac, the Jews went to Egypt, became slaves, and 430 years later came out "with a strong hand" (**Gen. 15:13-14; Exo. 12:40-42, 51; 13:3, 9, 14-16**). *The Israelites were slaves for 400 years and Joseph ruled for a portion of this time; hence, the 430 years.*

God's word to Daniel <u>predicted 5 World Empires</u> (**Dan. 2; 7**)–(1) Gold head and lion with eagle wings = Babylon (approx. 600-539 BC). (2) Silver chest/arms and bear with three ribs in its mouth = Medes and Persians (approx. 539-331 BC). (3) Brass belly/thighs and leopard with four heads and four wings = Greece (approx. 331-48 BC). 4) Iron legs and dreadful powerful beast = Rome (approx. 48 BC-364 AD), and (5), iron/clay feet = revived Roman Empire (coming soon).

God's Word also prophesied the <u>Fall of Nineveh</u> (**Isa. 10; Nah. 1-3**), the <u>Fall of Tyre</u> (**Eze. 26:1-21; Amos 1:9-10; Zec. 9:3-4**), Jesus <u>Christ's birth, life, sufferings, death, and Resurrection</u> (**Mat. 26:2, 26-28; Isa. 7:14; 9:6; 35:4-6; 53; Micah 5:2** and numerous more). *Additional prophecies may be seen at:* <u>*www.100prophecies.org*</u>.

Universal Appeal, Publication, Study, and Influence: <u>How many Bibles do you have</u> (1, 5, or more)? According to Barna Research Online, "The Bible," <u>www.barna.org</u>, studies completed in 1993, 92% of homes had one Bible and the average home in America had three. Most homes do not have multiple, or engraved leather bound versions of any other book.

The Bible is the <u>#1 published</u> book of all time, the <u>#1 studied</u> book of all time, the <u>#1 translated</u> book of all time. In fact, there are many languages in which the only written book is the Bible! There are more English translations alone. <u>How many Bible reference books</u> (paraphrases, translations, dictionaries, calendars, concordances, commentaries, maps, etc.) exist? <u>How many Biblical institutions or media are in operation</u> (clubs, centers, schools, churches, colleges, seminaries, radio and TV programs, DVDs, CDs, books, articles)? <u>How many governments, legislation, world empires</u> credit the Bible and belief in God as their basis? The Bible is <u>#1 quoted</u> Book. If the Bible were destroyed, it could be completely reconstructed by other books that quote it! *Interesting and intriguing Bible fun facts are found at:*

*http://christianteens.about.com/od/understandingyourbible/qt/Num
berFacts.htm.*

Archaeological Accuracy: Read anything in the Bible and research the archaeology of relatively recent discoveries related to Nineveh, Jericho, Babylon, Israel, the Temple, and the Universal Flood for a few examples of the archaeological accuracy of the scriptures.

Scientific Accuracy: Some contend that the Bible is intended for religion, but not for science. **Rev. 21:18, 21** describes heaven's streets as "<u>pure gold, like unto clear glass</u>" and "<u>pure gold, as it were transparent glass</u>". Scientists claimed for years that this was a scientific error in the Bible as they said gold was yellow-brown, but now that man's ability to purify gold has improved, they concede that Scripture was scientifically accurate. Purified gold becomes clear and transparent. **Isa. 40:22** describes the earth as spherical in seventh Century BC, "It is He Who sits above <u>the circle of the earth</u>." In times past scientists and others believed the earth was flat until centuries later, when scientists caught up. *A good reference site: http://www.clarifyingchristianity.com/science.shtml. Interesting Hebrew word for "circle" indicated spherical or arched, certainly not something flat or square. I do acknowledge historically the Catholic church did argue with Galileo and did force him to renounce his previously stated beliefs in the earth's shape, but that is not what God's Word said!* **Gen. 17:12** mandates <u>circumcision</u> to be when ("<u>he that is eight days old</u>"). It is now medically proven that the eighth day is best for clotting, the least pain, the best healing, fewer infections, etc.

Historical Accuracy: Look at Rome, Israel (land, law, allies, enemies, events . . .), clothes, husband and wife, marriage, weddings, divorce, remarriage, the family structure, births, burials, funerals, races, languages (**Gen. 11**), our current calendar (B.C.—"Before Christ" and A.D.—Anno Domini is Medieval Latin for "In the Year of our Lord"— our Lord refers to Jesus Christ).

Authority, Value, and Character—Reveals: <u>absolute truth</u>, <u>morality</u> (right and wrong, sin, and even a social, law, and legal framework), the <u>psychology of man</u>, the <u>purpose or meaning of life</u>, the <u>Person of Jesus Christ</u> (the God-Man), the <u>attributes, perfections, and nature of God</u>, <u>how to be saved</u> (now and eternally), and it has NEVER had any confirmed errors.

Preservation and Indestructibility: Many people and governments have tried to burn, ban, or destroy the Bible and have never succeeded (cf. **Mat. 5:18; 24:35; Mar. 13:31; Luk. 21:33**). I was told Voltaire said, "In 100 years this book will be forgotten, eliminated" and 50 years later (sadly Voltaire was dead and in hell) and the Geneva Bible Society was printing and distributing Bibles with his home as the headquarters. *See others attempts mentioned under "5—Preservation" of God's progressively revealed Word.*

Power to change lives: Millions of people attest to changed lives as a result of reading the Word of God. The apostles, the founding fathers, the Church fathers, kings, presidents, men, women, boys, and girls make this claim. The most influential Book was endorsed by the most influential Person, Jesus Christ. Consider its effect on society as abusers, alcoholics, drug users, homosexuals, prostitutes, murderers, etc., who have become some of the most giving, productive, and humble servants of Christ (c.f. **Rom. 1:16-17; Heb. 4:12**). Has any other book that power? Has any other book had such a profound impact? D.L. Moody once asserted that t*he Bible was not given to increase our knowledge, but to change our lives.*

The Nation of Israel: The Bible is the most complete Book of Israel's past, present, and future (history, reign, moral, ceremonial, and legislative law, warfare, suffering, captivity, freedom, spanning thousands of years). The OT is the tender history of God speaking to, working through, revealing Himself to, proclaiming His Son Jesus to His chosen people Israel, the Jews!

Other books claiming to be "Sacred": Compare the Bible with the Koran, Vedas, book of Mormon, Apocrypha, writings of Confucius, et al. Not one of these works even comes close to any evidence of Divine authorship. The facts are that most of these are quite poor in quality and thus, have appealed to the uneducated and have been promulgated or forced by governments, cults, or sects. Compare internal statements about themselves, continuity, depth, accuracy, prophecy, study, publication, influence, archaeological, Historical, scientific, value, indestructibility, power to transform, the nation of Israel and other secular statements of Israel concurrence. Then read some of the absurdities of these other "so-called" "sacred" writings. *There is no comparison, and on this point, historians and linguists must agree.*

How to Study the Bible (3 Major Steps)

Approach the study of God's Word reverently, humbly, and prayerfully. (**2Ti. 2:15; Heb. 4:12**). The three steps to follow are not a formula, but a process (for a lifetime of study). Study necessitates consistency and discipline. It is critical to not reverse or mix up these steps as each step builds and is dependent on the previous step.

1—Observation (Seeing): <u>What does it say</u>? Literally what is the subject, verb, object, singular, plural, tenses, main point, thesis, conclusion, repetition, emphasis, word order and usage, style. There should be no spiritualizing, or allegories assigned, unless it says this is an allegory, e.g. **Gal. 4:24**. <u>Terms</u>—word definitions and usage. <u>Structure</u>—grammatical, literary, arrangement, introduction, climax, conclusion, parallelism, class conditions, positive/negative answers, rhythm/rhyme, acrostics, <u>literary form</u> (narrative, etc), Q&A, rhetorical, poetic, psalms/songs, wisdom, prophetic, epistolary, apocalyptic, idioms, figures of Speech, <u>atmosphere/tone</u>-sarcastic, romantic, harsh, light, thankful, sad, positive, negative, or humorous. Meditation and memorization are great observation techniques to find more than was originally seen. Read, re-read, and read again. Then come back and read again later. Listen to Scripture while sleeping to let your mind observe more, brainwash, and impact your subconscious and dreams. Act as a reporter asking the questions <u>W</u>ho, <u>W</u>hat, <u>W</u>hen, <u>W</u>here, and <u>W</u>hy? These should be stated reasons only, not ones imposed by the reader. The Greek "hina" clause denotes purpose, "<u>that</u> your joy may be full." The reason we should ask is stated (cf. **Joh. 16:24**). If the reason is not stated, it is not an observation; the "Why" then becomes an interpretation...

Observation is best by first hand exposure to Gods Word. Think for yourself, it will help you (1) Prepare your thoughts for others, (2) Fall in love with the Author, and (3) Get the joy of self-discovery. One has said, "The mind is like a Parachute, it only works when it is open." God will "open your eyes", if that is your prayer when you approach His Word for study. Avoid bringing preconceived ideas to what the passage says or means. Look at God's Word and truly see what God says, not what the reader wants Him to say. Everyone has baggage, or preconceived notions from childhood or other impressions from previous study or writings. Try to leave these ideas behind when you read God's Word. Listen to God, not the world, or the culture. Every time you read the Bible, determine to read it as if reading for the first time. **Gal. 4:24** is the only place an allegory is mentioned in the Bible, and it tells us specifically what and how these types are allegorical. Anything else that is added or taken away from the allegory makes it man's not God Word. **Rev. 17:18** says, "And the woman which thou sawest is that great city, which reigneth over the kings of the earth." Again, it tells us the symbol or representation. It doesn't move to the interpretation phase or let everyone guess their own interpretation, or meaning of Scripture. *> Time in Observation = < Time in Interpretation (and Interpretations will = > Accuracy). The secret to an effective public ministry is an effective private one with God in His Word. There is no shortcut for time spent in God's Word.*

2—Interpretation (Understanding): <u>What does it mean</u>? Found in <u>Observations</u>—What does it say? <u>Audience</u>—To whom is it written? <u>Context</u>—Where is it found and what is around it? <u>Historical Setting</u>—What is, has, or will occur? <u>Background</u>—What is the location? <u>Date</u>—when was it written, or what is the time period? Inspired <u>Writer</u>—Who wrote and what was his occupation, family situation, style, and why were they chosen? <u>Purpose/Occasion</u>— What is the stated reason for writing? <u>Comparison</u>—What does God say in the rest of the Bible about this? **CROSS**-<u>References</u>—What other passages shed light? <u>Consultation</u>—What views do others have? <u>Literally</u> apply the rules of <u>grammar</u> and <u>syntax</u>. <u>Meaning is determined by what was said</u> in the content and context, <u>not by what the reader thinks God may have intended to say</u>, but didn't say with the inspired words. Use the searching "C" words: Content, Context, Comparison, and Consultation for clarity and accuracy.

Some specific examples are listed below. **John 15:5**: "You are the branches." This is a literal metaphor (comparing people to branches on a vine). **Judges 16:12**: Samson broke the rope "like a thread." This is a literal simile (a comparison of Samson's strength, strong enough to make a strong rope appear as weak as a thread). *Understand it literally as written, don't add your own "symbolism" to fit what you wish it said (that is theological baggage, which we all have). Use the rules of literature to understand what was written. This allows God through His Word to be the authority, and not you (as the reader) determining what it means.*

Hermeneutics is the art and science of textual interpretation. Below is a commonly misinterpreted passage. By applying these literal hermeneutical processes it is easy to see what this passages means. **Matthew 7:1** says, "Judge not, that you be not judged." What does that mean? Many believe it means you shouldn't judge others. Is that what it means? *Start with the 4—Cs briefly summarized.* **Content**—Judging. **Context**—Sermon on the Mount (**Mat. 5-7**). Understand others will judge you with the severity with which you judge them (**7:1**). Clean up your own life/sin before helping others (**7:3-5**). Don't judge the unsaved because they won't understand or appreciate and will attack you (**7:6**). Don't be hypocritical; judge self first (so you're not a hypocrite). The Golden Rule (**7:12**)—Treating others the way you want to be treated when you have sin, forgiving sins, not always judging (**Luk. 6:37**). Recognizing the saved versus unsaved by judging their fruit or works (**7:15-20**). **Comparison**—1Co. **2:15; 5:12-13; 6:1-8; Luk. 6:37; Rom. 2:1-2; 14; 1Co. 4:3-5; Jam. 4:11-12**, etc. **Consultation**—Love, forgive, judge self first; Judge to help others, not condemning; not wasting time by judging unsaved, focus on getting them to see their need for salvation. *God's Word will NEVER contradict itself. Seeming contradictions are always opportunities for deeper learning and deeper study.*

Some consider correlation a part of Interpretation as a fifth "C;" others separate it into a fourth step, and some place it in between

Interpretation or Application. **Correlation (Integrating):** Where does it fit? Harmonize multiple passages by correlating or integrating multiple interpretations. This needs to be a key conscious step (while interpreting or applying). Placing correlation here as an outgrowth of interpretation seems to support the process best, but it is sometimes "felt" or seen during application. Each step frequently cycles the student back thru each step. Some common correlation related groupings are called: Biblical Theology (Scripturally integrated cross references), Systematic Theology (Scripture + rationale + other truth; e.g., historical, philosophical, scientific, and archaeological), Biblical worldview (social, political, cultural thought processes...), chronology/timelines (sequencing or ordering events), and topical or thematic (similar to Systematic Theology, but at a smaller topic level).

3—Application (Implementing): How does this change my life? What is God's purpose for me from His Word? What should I think, remember, be, do, or say differently? Think through what you have learned daily, weekly, monthly, yearly, and in your lifetime. There are many observations, one meaning in interpretation, and many applications. Dr. Howard Hendricks said, "*Observation and Interpretation, without Application is like an Abortion.*" You defeat the whole purpose of seeing and understanding—it is to change us and conform us to the glory and image of Christ, so that we can have an abundant life now. Application is practicing and obeying what you've learned. **James 1:22-25** says, "But be ye doers of the Word, and not hearers only, deceiving your own selves. For if any be a hearer of the Word, and not a doer, he is like unto a man beholding his natural face in a glass: For he beholdeth himself, and goeth his way, and straightway forgetteth what manner of man he was. But whoso looketh into the perfect law of liberty, and continueth therein, he being not a forgetful hearer, but a doer of the work, this man shall be blessed in his deed." The Word of God is conforming you as you study it. Four application actions: (1) Know (yourself and situation), (2) Relate (thoughts, feelings, decisions, home, school, Church, socially, work), (3) Meditate, and (4) Practice (Is this a truth to know, believe, or embrace? Is there a sin to forsake, a command to obey, an example to follow? *God's Word was not written to* *merely inform, but to change! It doesn't matter how much you know (or think you know); it matters how much you apply.*

A piece of application, and applying and obeying, is communication. It includes homiletics (assembling the principles of rhetoric for public communications for preaching, teaching, and evangelism). **Communication (Sharing)**: How can I effectively share this with others? This is where you demonstrate, overflow, share, teach, or preach God's Word as commanded. **2Ti. 2:24** says, "the servant of the Lord must . . . be . . . apt to teach", **Gal. 6:6** says, "Let him that is taught in the word communicate unto him that teaches in all good things." **2Ti. 4:2** says, "Preach the word; be instant in season, out of season; reprove, rebuke, exhort with all longsuffering and doctrine." My "Top 10 Ways to Communicate God's Word" or assist others in applying God's Word are listed below.

1. Target the audience's spiritual condition (If unknown, always assume both saved and unsaved are present; so, always present the simple gospel. For a primarily unsaved audience, focus on salvation. For a saved audience, focus on spiritual growth).
2. Leverage what you have learned (You can't effectively share what is not real in your life; learn a lesson before teaching it).
3. Learn from other learners (As you share and interact you'll learn more and gain better clarity).
4. Prayer (Begin study and sharing with prayer while asking God to teach you and prepare the hearer's hearts—This is according to His will and He promises He will answer; cf. **Joh. 16:23-24**).
5. Use a hook (This brings the Bible where your audience lives, feels, and needs. Use humor, stories, relating deep spiritual truths where the learner lives).
6. Quote Scripture directly, read, or play it. It will "never return void," and it will always be used by the Holy Spirit).
7. Provide direct interaction when possible. Use questions, get students involved with God's Word to see the joy of discovery, making God's truth, their truth).
8. Encourage decisions. Guide students to make decisions based upon the truths of God's Word and commands. Many have said

that no one ever asked or invited them to accept Christ and His teachings.

9. Scriptural thoroughness (Try not to avoid Scripture because it not popular or palatable. Consistently try to teach the full counsel of God; His complete Word).

10. Focus on learner applications (Engage learners in seeing specific practical ways to apply directly in their life. That's when change happens).

The example of Jeremiah raises the consciousness of the teacher in communicating God's Word to those in need. **Jer. 20:9** *says, "Then I said, I will not make mention of Him, nor speak any more in His name. But his Word was in mine heart as a burning fire shut up in my bones, and I was weary with forbearing, and I could not stay."*

Select Tools for Effective Bible Study

Tools can be used for one or more of the Bible study steps. It is best to start with God's Word and allow the Holy Spirit to speak to you alone. After some reading and studying on your own, then take time listen to others. All truth is God's truth, and God wants to communicate His truth to us. There are many online tools to assist in Bible study. Some top tools are listed below:

1. **Dictionaries**—in your primary language and in the same language as your Bible (e.g., Webster's and others).

2. **Exhaustive Concordance**—to understand word meanings in the Bible's original written languages for greater precision (e.g. Strong's Concordance with Hebrew and Greek Lexicon).

3. **Bible versions, topical, interlinear (Bibles that show the Greek and/or Hebrew text), and comparison Bibles.** The NKJV, KJV, NASB, NIV are excellent comparisons to see minor translation differences.

4. **Commentaries and Bible dictionaries**—learn from the study of others, e.g., notes from Study Bibles like Ryrie, Scofield, MacArthur, David Jeremiah, Matthew Henry, Thompson, et al).

5. **Maps and encyclopedias**—cover Biblical and modern times (geographical, historical, and cultural studies that help provide context and a better understanding of regions then and now).

6. **Bible paraphrases**—provide other perspectives on its meaning; Exercise caution because these are not God's Word, only man's restating of God's Word.
7. **Books, sermons, classes, poems, internet, media, charts, outlines**—these provide other perspectives and practical application if used with discernment. There are many false teachers.

7 Great Free Bible Tools

1. www.onlinebible.org (Online Bible—downloadable Bible program, view, search, versions, translations, languages, exhaustive concordances, notes, commentaries)
2. www.esword.net (eSword Bible—downloadable Bible Program, view, search, versions, translations, languages, exhaustive concordances, notes, commentaries)
3. www.audiotreasure.com (Audio downloadable Bible in mp3)
4. www.blueletterbible.org (Blue Letter Bible—Online Bible program, view, search, versions, translations, languages, exhaustive concordances, notes, commentaries)
5. bibleapps.com/strongs.htm (Strong's Exhaustive Concordance— online Hebrew and Greek dictionary to show original Hebrew and Greek words in your language).
6. www.biblestudytools.com (Bible study site—online Bible verse searches and display in 30+ different Bible translations, in-depth studies, commentaries, encyclopedias, etc.)
7. www.merriam-webster.com (Merriam-Webster Online—online dictionary and thesaurus).

The single most powerful, intelligent, fastest eternal super person ever, Who created and sustains everything and everyone for His own purpose, and deserves our highest love and admiration.

Introduction

Theology Proper comes from the Greek stems *"Theos"*, meaning God, and *"logos"*, meaning a word about, the science of, or the study of; thus **Theology Proper is the study of God the Father**. Some key verses are **Gen. 1:1** and **Deu. 6:4-5**. **Genesis 1:1** says, "In the beginning God created the heaven and the earth." **Deu. 6:4-5** says, "Hear, O Israel: The LORD our God *is* one LORD: And thou shalt love the LORD thy God with all thine heart, and with all thy soul, and with all thy might."

Existence—Scripturally Seen

God is Scripturally assumed, stated, and explained in many passages, starting in the first verse in the Bible. "In the beginning God . . ." (**Gen. 1:1**). "But without faith it is impossible to please Him: for he that cometh to God must believe that He is, and that He is a rewarder of them that diligently seek Him." (**Heb. 11:6**). Out of the numerous names for God, just "LORD" and "God" occur 9,161 times in the Bible. **Romans 1:19-25, 28** says, "Because that which may be known of God is manifest in them; for God hath shewed *it* unto them. For the invisible things of him from the creation of the world are clearly seen, being understood by the things that are made, *even* his eternal power and Godhead; so that they are without excuse: Because that, when they knew God, they glorified *him* not as God, neither were thankful; but became vain in their imaginations, and their foolish heart was darkened. Professing themselves to be wise, they became fools, And changed the glory of the incorruptible God into an image made like to corruptible man, and to birds, and four-footed beasts, and creeping things. Wherefore God also gave them up to uncleanness through the lusts of their own hearts, to dishonor their own bodies between themselves: Who changed the truth of God into a lie, and worshipped and served the creature more than the Creator, who is blessed forever. Amen. And even as they did not like to retain God in *their* knowledge, God gave them over to a

24

reprobate mind, to do those things which are not convenient;" "The fool has said in his heart, There is no God." (**Psa. 14:1**; **53:1**).

Existence—Rationally Seen

God is rationally seen through man's reason, rational arguments, and man's intellect. Let's start with some "A Posteriori" or Inductive rational arguments or reasoning from specific to general.

Cosmological (1st Cause): Every effect must have a sufficient cause; the cosmos or universe is quite an effect, which must imply a sufficient cause...thus God. Sometimes this is referred to as *Cause and Effect* (**Heb. 11:3**; **Isa. 40:26-28**; **Act. 14:15-17**; **17:24f**; **Psa. 19**). It is interesting that many believe in a "Big Bang", but don't give a thought about Who was, and is the "Big Banger" (see Anthropology).

Anthropological or Moral (Personal 1st Cause): The uniqueness of the intellectual, emotional, and volitional nature of man and his existence is unexplainable apart from a similar, yet greater being...thus God. Morality, reason, and the conscience are unexplained apart from God, or sometimes referred to as *Mankind's Uniqueness* (**Rom. 1:19-2:16**; **Psa. 8**; **Gen. 1:26-27**).

Teleological (Rational 1st Cause): This is often called *Intelligent Design*. Intelligent Design implies and requires an appropriate designer, thus God. Look at the stars, planets, nature, a snowflake, our body, fingerprints, IRIS, a leaf, a single cell, DNA. Simple reason says that if you find even a simple a gold watch opened with only five synchronized gears keeping time in the desert that your first rational thought is not that there was an accidental gold ore explosion creating a watch. Even the ignorant and uneducated reason this watch came from a watch designer and maker, not an unintelligent, accidental, unexplained explosion.

The second type of rationale arguments are called "A priori" or Deductive reasoning from general to specific. These are the opposite type of reasoning from the "A Posteriori" reasoning.

Ontological (Perfect 1ˢᵗ Cause): The *Universal Belief* in a Supreme Being or God (historically, as well as today and even trans-culturally) necessitates the existence of God. Sometimes this is referred to as **Intuitional** or **1ˢᵗ Truths**. *Who do people call for when they are about to die? It is said that there are no "Atheists" on their death bed.*

Eclectically or Congruity (Reasonable Cause): The weight of combining these logical arguments of Cause and Effect, Man's Unique Nature and Existence, Design Implies a Designer, the Universal Belief in God, the Scriptural Proof, and the fact that there is no proof at all to the contrary makes the existence of God most reasonable.

Alternatives: The Big Bang, Swiss Cheese, String Theories, etc. are all unreasonable, and there really isn't one intelligent or intellectually honest alternative to God. Not many scientists really believe these **unproven and irrational theories**, but many have tenure and grant pressure to be silent in their profession. *Are you ready to hear the best theory against an eternal personal God Who created man in His own image? Here it is: Something, somehow, somewhere, eternally existed, but changed, maybe exploded, and denied the universal laws of science observed today (2ⁿᵈ Law of Thermodynamics—things are breaking down, and abiogenesis—life can't come from non-life), kept getting better until man appeared (even the immaterial soul, mind, and spirit), and then all the evidence disappeared. Additionally, there are no missing link fossils (can't even find one), and this nonsense isn't consistent with the demands of the scientific method (observable, measurable, and repeatable). This best theory against God takes trillions of years (because with enough time it might be possible). Wow, what faith these naturalistic atheists must have! Why does believing in God make so much more sense than the alternatives? Simply, it is true!*

<u>Existence—Seen by the Unexplainable</u>
The unexplainable is unexplained, apart from God's existence. Some of those unexplainable things are: <u>The Bible</u> (the most influential, published, translated, studied, quoted, popular Book); <u>Jesus Christ</u> (the most influential, unique, awesome, revered, worshipped,

Person); <u>Science</u> (Creation versus the alternatives, e.g. Evolution); <u>Millions of Changed lives</u> (the experience of nations, institutions, Churches, individuals that are addicted to drugs, sex, alcohol, self-pleasure, and then turn to loving and giving); the <u>Occult or Supernatural</u> (spirits, ghosts, demons, angels); <u>Miracles</u> (unnatural, unexplainable by Science); <u>Curse Words</u> ("Jesus Christ", "God" this or that—Incidentally, you don't hear people yelling the names of Buddha, Confucius, Mohammed); the <u>Nation of Israel</u> (Why is this nation so special, but so small? How did they again become a nation? How did they become so persecuted as God's people that there is even a word "anti-Semitism"?); and <u>History</u> (see how God and His ways are proven because of God's Sovereign involvement and truth through cultures around the world, including the great country America).

Existence—Seen by Top Alternatives

The top alternatives / theories have so many holes. There simply are no credible theories, belief systems, or religions that even come close to a belief in <u>Theism</u>—a personal God or <u>Monotheism</u>—one Supreme Being, God. Some of the shallow belief systems, false religions, or cults (all man made) can be summarized into these categories: <u>Atheism</u>—Atheism is a belief in no God, and includes most naturalistic theories, or science without God; <u>Agnosticism</u>—Agnosticism is a belief that no one can know if God exists (The agnostic lives like an atheist, but is unsure and rarely searches for answers. Usually the agnostic doesn't believe in absolutes of any kind. Ironically, the agnostic knows for sure that no one can know; Furthermore, agnostics are absolutely sure that there are no absolutes); <u>Deism</u>—Deism is the belief that God started it all, but is not personally involved in maintaining the world or intervening in it (really deny God in their life or any purpose to their own besides temporary pleasure); <u>Dualism</u>—Dualism is the belief that two gods, one good and one bad, are supposedly equal in power and persuasion and are perhaps opposing forces drifting away from a Supreme God towards two powerful influences); <u>Tri-theism</u>—Tri-theism is a belief that three Gods exist that are equal in power, though this idea is less common, it sometimes is just a demonstration of a lack of understanding of Trinitarian thinking

regarding a true Triune God; see section to come); Polytheism—
Polytheism is a belief in many gods, popular in Greek mythology to
emphasize an extreme of a specific attribute; Pantheism—Pantheism
is a belief that God is everything. While this theory recognizes God's
immensity, it minimizes God by making Him everything, and
therefore unique in nothing; Panentheism—Panentheism is the
belief that God is in everything. This belief recognizes God's
omnipresence, but makes Him impersonal, good and bad and not
personal.

If God doesn't exist and you believe in Him, no problem (you're a
better citizen); if God does exist and you do not believe in Him and
what He says about Hell (an everlasting place of burning judgment),
then big problem. Is it worth risking all eternity in such torment?

God's Attributes, Perfections, Characteristics, Quality, or Nature
If monotheism makes the most sense and provides the least eternal
risk and one could argue produces the best citizens, Who is God and
what can be known of Him? **Deu. 29:29**: "The secret things belong
unto the LORD our God: but those things which are revealed belong
unto us and to our children forever, that we may do all the words of
this law." **Dan. 2:22**: "He revealeth the deep and secret things: He
knoweth what is in the darkness, and the light dwelleth with Him."
Phi. 3:10: "That I may know Him . . ." Merriam-Webster (www.m-
w.org) defines an attribute as: "1: an inherent characteristic; also: an
accidental quality; 2: an object closely associated with or belonging
to a specific person, thing, or office <a scepter is the attribute of
power>; especially: such an object used for identification in painting
or sculpture; 3: a word ascribing a quality; especially: adjective".

Natural or Incommunicable Attributes
God is much bigger than any of us imagine. When our view of Him is
small, our problems loom large. The bigger and better your view of
God, the more accurate your perspective becomes (and the smaller
your problems will seem). There are two primary types of attributes
when describing God. The first category includes natural or
incommunicable. These are supernatural or those that should cause
worship; those attributes mankind cannot evidence. These natural

or incommunicable attributes are the following: <u>Self-Existence (life)</u>—He is the **uncaused** One; He is the only completely **independent** One; He is completely **free** (**Isa. 40:13 - 14**; **Joh. 5:26**; **14:6**; **1Jo. 5:20**). <u>Infinity</u> or Infinitude—**He is not limited**, and is only bound by His nature (**Psa. 90:2**; **145:3**). <u>Eternality</u>—He is not limited by **time** (**Deu. 32:40**; **1Ti. 6:16**; **Rev. 4:8**). <u>Immensity</u>—He is not limited by **space** (omnipresence). <u>Sovereignty</u>—He is unlimited by **events** (**complete control** or rule; **Jer.31:1**; **32:27**; **Jos. 3:13**; **Eph. 1:11**; **Gen. 50:20**—even over evil). <u>Spirituality</u> (Incorporeal)–He is, of course **invisible**, without material substance (**Joh. 4:24**; therefore **Joh. 1:18**). <u>Immutability</u>–**He is absolutely unchangeable** in being or essence (**Mal. 3:6**; **Psa. 102:26-27**; **James 1:17**). <u>Omniscience</u>—**He is all knowing** and understanding, including possible or actual, past, present, and future. He has perfect knowledge and foreknowledge (**Psa. 139:4**; **147:4-5**; **Job 37:16**; **1Jo. 3:20**; **Isa. 40:13, 14, 28**; **65:24**; **Mat. 9:4**; **10:30**; **Rom. 11:33**; **Heb. 4:13**). This includes knowledge without having to discover facts, since God **never learns anything**; and knowledge that is complete and inclusive since God **always knows everything**. Omniscience examples include: **Psa. 147:5**—". . . His understanding is infinite." **Job 37:16**—". . . Him which is perfect in knowledge?" **1Jo. 3:20**—". . . God is greater than our heart, and knoweth all things." **Rom. 11:33**: "O the depth of the riches both of the wisdom and knowledge of God! How unsearchable are His judgments, and His ways past finding out!" <u>Omnipresence</u>—In His omnipresence He is personally present everywhere at once in His entirety, **transcending even spatial limitations**), and includes His immensity, immanence, and transcendence (**Jer. 23:24**; **Psa. 139:5-13**; cf. **Deu. 31:6**; **Heb. 13:5**; **Psa. 23:4**; **Deu. 4:39**; **Isa. 43:2**; **66:1**; **Jer. 23:23-24**; **Act. 17:27**; **Amo. 9:2**). **Psa. 139:7-10**—"Whither shall I go from Thy Spirit? Or whither shall I flee from Thy presence? If I ascend up into heaven, Thou art there: if I make my bed in Hell, behold, Thou art there. If I take the wings of the morning, and dwell in the uttermost parts of the sea; Even there shall Thy hand lead me, and Thy right hand shall hold me." This is in direct opposition to the ideologies that: parts of Him are everywhere, a mere material presence, pantheism (God is everything) or panentheism (God is in everything). *Deu. 31:6—"Be strong and of a good courage, fear not, nor be afraid of them: for the LORD thy God, <u>He it is that doth go</u>*

with thee; He will not fail thee, nor forsake thee." **Heb. 13:5**—"*. . . I will never leave thee, nor forsake thee.*" **Psa. 23:4**—"*. . . I will fear no evil: for thou art with me . . .*" *God is right where you need Him, always. You are always in His presence. Embrace Him, and come boldly unto Him (**Heb. 4:16**). Spurgeon tells a story of an atheist newspaper writer who wrote an article stating, "God is NO WHERE." While the father was forcing his child to read the headline the son read, "God is NOW HERE." In that single moment of time, God pierced his own heart with the truth of His certain omnipresence.*

Omnipotence—God is **All - powerful,** or unlimited in power (**Rev. 19:6**; **Mat. 19:26**; **Jer. 32:17**; **Gen. 1**; **18:14**; **Heb. 1:3**; **Psa. 33:9**; **Rev. 19:6**). He is Almighty, as evidenced in His Divine creation and the preservation of it, His resurrection, His salvation, and His Divine judgment. He is able! **Rev. 19:6-7**—" . . . Alleluia: for the Lord God omnipotent reigneth. Let us be glad and rejoice, and give honor to Him . . ." Jer. *32:17*—*"Ah Lord GOD! Behold, Thou hast made the heaven and the earth by Thy **great power** and stretched out arm, and there is nothing too hard for Thee."* **Mat. 19:26**— *". . . With men this is impossible; but **with God all things are possible**."* *The Greek adjective "pantokrator" is translated "omnipotent" in* **Rev. 19:6**, *but translated* **"Almighty"** *(KJV) the other nine times (**2Cor 6:18**; **Rev 1:8**; **4:8**; **11:17**; **15:3**; **16:7, 14**; **19:15**; **21:22**). Although "Sovereignty" is placed here under Infinity, the unlimited "Authority" and "Power" (Greek dunatos) also clearly are seen in God's omnipotence. God's names also demonstrate His omnipotence. God Almighty (Hebrew El Shaddai),* **1Co. 15:24-25**— *"Then cometh the end, when He shall have delivered up the kingdom to God, even the Father; when He shall have put down **all rule and all authority and power**. For **He must reign**, till He hath put all enemies under His feet."* *No matter what a person faces, even death, He is able, He has the power, He has the authority "to do above what you ask or think." George Frederich Handel composed the great "Hallelujah Chorus" (**Rev. 19:6-7**). That is why King George II stood at the premiere of" Handel's Messiah"; he recognized the truth about our All Powerful God (presented straight from Scripture). All will obey this truth, even if not here on earth, as "every knee shall bow and every tongue confess" (**Isa. 45:23**; **Rom. 14:11**; **Php. 2:11**) one day before God's sovereign ruling throne.*

30

Moral or Communicable Attributes

The second type of God's attributes is called moral or communicable. These are characterized in this way because mankind may evidence these characteristics and be conformed to God, or become like Him. Love—Concern, care, compassion, "**God is love.**" Love is the greatest commandment (1st and 2nd) and completely fulfills the Law (**1Jo. 4:7-8, 12, 16; Rom. 5:8; 13:10; Mat. 12:37-39; Gal. 5:14**). *There are three main Greek words for love: (1) "**Agape**," which is God's love or an unconditional type love; (2) "**Phileo**," which is brotherly, sisterly, or friendship type love; (3) "**Eros**," which is erotic, sexual, or lustful type love.* **Mat. 12:37-39**—*"Jesus said unto him, Thou shalt love the Lord thy God with all thy heart, and with all thy soul, and with all thy mind. This is **the first and great commandment**. And **the second** is like unto it, Thou shalt **love thy neighbor as thyself**." **Gal. 5:14**—"For **all the law is fulfilled** in one word, even in this; Thou shalt love thy neighbor as thyself." **Rom. 13:10**—"Love worketh no ill to his neighbor: therefore **love is the fulfilling of the law**." **1Jo. 4:7-8, 12, 16, 19**—"Beloved, let us love one another: for **love is of God**; and **every one that loveth is born of God**, and **knoweth God**. He that loveth not knoweth not God; for **God is love**. No man hath seen God at any time. If we love one another, God dwelleth in us, and **His love is perfected in us**. And we have known and believed the love that God hath to us. **God is love**; and he that dwelleth in love dwelleth in God, and God in him: No man hath seen God at any time. **If we love one another, God dwelleth in us**, and His love is perfected in us. **We love Him, because He first loved us**." We get to see what God is like when we love perfectly. God dwells in us when we love. We should respond to His love by loving.* **1Co. 13:4-8a** *is **the Great Love Chapter** that helps us understand God's agape love (8 positives "+" and 8 negatives "-").*

Love Is (+)	Love Is Not (-)
Patient (long suffering)	Envious (jealous*)
Kind	Vaunting itself (boasting)
Rejoicing in the truth	Puffed up (proud)
Bearing (covering) all things (protects)	Behaving unseemly (rude)
Believing all things (trusts/thinks best)	Seeking its own (selfish)
Hoping all things (hopes)	Easily provoked (angered)
Enduring all things (perseveres)	Thinking any evil (keeping record)
Never failing (perseveres; eternal)	Rejoicing in iniquity (delight in evil)

*God is not jealous in a bad way, but for our good, cf. **Nah. 1:2***

Mercy—Withholding of judgment, patient, long-suffering, forgiving; *not giving what is deserved*; "**God is merciful**"; "**His mercy endures forever**" (**Num. 14:18; Psa. 103:8; 116:5; 136; 145:8; Rom. 11:32; Ti. 3:5**). **Num. 14:18**—"The LORD is longsuffering, and **of great mercy, forgiving iniquity** . . ."

Grace—Giving of unmerited, undeserved favor; kind. *Giving what is not deserved.* "**God is gracious**"; "**God is good**"; "**He gives more grace**" (**Exo. 34:6; 2Ch. 30:9; Neh. 9:17; Jonah 4:2; Eph. 2:8-9; Psa. 34:8; 73:1; Jam. 1:17; 1Ti. 4:4; Jam. 4:6; 1Pe. 4:10**). **1Pe. 4:10**—"As **every man hath received the gift**, even so minister the same one to another, as good stewards **of the manifold grace of God**." **Rom. 5:17, 20**—"For if by one man's offence death reigned by one; much more they which receive **abundance of grace** and of **the gift** of righteousness shall reign in life by one, Jesus Christ). Moreover the law entered, that the offence might abound. But where sin abounded, **grace did much more abound**"

Holiness—**Absolute perfection**; separate from sin or evil (**Lev. 11:44-45; 19:2; 1Ch. 16:29; Isa. 6:3; 1Pe. 1:16; Rev. 4:8; Psa. 19:7; Mat. 5:48; Jam. 1:13**). **Isa. 6:3**—". . . **Holy, holy, holy, is the LORD** of hosts, the whole earth is full of his glory." **Hab. 1:13**—"Thou art of **purer eyes than to behold evil**, and **canst not look on iniquity** . . ." **1Pe. 1:16**—". . . Be ye holy; for **I am holy**." The two main aspects to holiness are righteousness and Justice. Righteousness is God's standard of perfection (His Person and Law). "**God is righteous**"; "**the Lord is perfect**"; "**God is light**" (**Dan. 9:14; Mat. 5:48; Psa. 19:7; Rev. 16:7; 1Jo. 1:5**). *Righteousness is not just the absence of sin; it is the presence of perfection. Sin is anything less than 0 down to 100% sinfulness or evil. Righteousness is anything greater than 0 up to 100%. Righteousness is as far above 0 as Sin is below it. God's Holiness or Righteousness is always perfect (100%+).*

Justice—**Fairness**; not violating God's righteousness, implementing it; "**He is just**" (**Job 34:17; Isa. 45:21; Zep. 3:5; Zec. 9:9; Rom. 3:26**); **Moral Equality**—"**God is no respecter of persons**" (**Deu. 32:4; Acts**

10:34; 2Chr. 19:7; Rom. 2:11; Eph. 6:9; 1Pe. 1:17); "**God is a consuming fire**" (**Heb. 12:29**). *Follow God and as* **Pro. 29:9** *says, "Then shall you understand righteousness, and judgment, and equity; yea, every good path."*

Unity—One God (**Deu. 6:4; Mar. 12:32; 1Co. 8:6; Eph. 4:6**). Truth— Perfect **alignment with reality; no error, no deception**, and **no lie.** Fact, fidelity, faithful, consistent, constant, reliable (**Job 3:33; 2Co. 1:18; Joh. 14:6; Heb. 6:18**); "**God is true**" (**Joh. 3:33; 2Co. 1:18**)

Faithful—Adheres to promises; steadfast to standard, to truth, in affection; loyal (see Hebrew-Checed, Hesed - loyal love, mercies); gives strong assurance (**2Ti. 2:12-13; 2Th. 3:3**); "**God is faithful**" (**1Co. 1:9; 10:13**). *Some theologians do not show unity or truth as attributes; some include more from the definitions. Unity is true of almost any person. Truth could have been included with immutability, as it doesn't change; or included with omniscience, as God knows all truth; hence, a person is faithful if they remain true to their promises.*

Descriptions of God, the Lord

"**God is...**" These are not attributes, not names, but descriptions of God, or His actions. Each are listed in order and exactly quoted as progressively revealed about God in Scripture. *These descriptions may include names or attributes.* The Bible says numerous times that "God is . . ." *Below are* some of the most meaningful attributes and descriptions, exactly quoted. *Read, worship, and be encouraged as you see a more complete revelation of our awesome God.*

"God is" Witness (**Gen. 31:50; 1Th. 2:5**), A consuming fire (**Deu. 4:24; 9:23; Heb. 12:29**), Merciful (**Deu. 4:31; Psa. 116:5**), One LORD (**Deu. 6:4; Mar. 12:29**), A Jealous God (**Deu. 4:24; 6:25**), God of gods, Lord of Lords, a Great God, a Mighty, a Terrible (**Deu. 10:17**), Your Refuge (**Deu. 33:27**), My Strength and Power (**2Sa. 22:33; Hab. 3:19**), Gracious (**2Ch. 30:9**), Greater (**Job 33:12; Luk. 7:28; 1Jo. 3:20; 5:9**), Mighty (**Job 36:5**), Great (**Job 36:26**), Terrible Majesty (**Job 37:22**), Angry with the wicked every day (**Psa. 7:11**), The LORD (**Psa. 33:12; 118:27; 144:15**), Our Refuge and Strength (**Psa. 46:1**), The King of all the earth (**Psa. 47:7**), Known (**Psa. 48:3**), Our God (**Psa. 48:14**), Judge (**Psa. 50:6**), My Helper (**Psa. 54:4**), For Me (**Psa. 56:9**), My Defense (**Psa. 59:9, 17**), My Salvation and My Glory (**Psa. 62:7; Isa. 12:2**), A Refuge (**Psa. 62:8**), The God of Salvation (**Psa. 68:20**), Very High (**Psa. 71:19**), Good (**Psa. 73:1; 1Ti. 4:4**), The strength of my heart and my portion (**Psa. 73:26**), My King (**Psa. 74:12**), The Judge (**Psa. 75:7**), A Sun and Shield (**Psa. 84:11**), Greatly to be Feared . . . Reverence (**Psa. 89:7**), The Rock of My Refuge (**Psa. 94:22**), Holy (**Psa. 99:9; 1Co. 3:17**), In the Heavens (**Psa. 115:3**), Pure *(the Word of)* (**Pro. 30:5**), In Heaven (**Ecc. 5:2**), The Salvation of Israel (**Jer. 3:23**), A God of gods, Lord of Kings, A Revealer of Secrets (**Dan. 2:47**), Your God (**Dan. 6:20**), Righteous (**Dan. 9:14**), Jealous (**Nah. 1:2**), Able (**Mat. 3:9; Luk. 3:8; Rom. 11:23; 14:4; 2Co. 9:8**), True (**Joh. 3:33; 1Co. 1:18**), A Spirit (**Joh. 4:24**), He which . . . Giveth Life (**Joh. 6:33**), Glorified (**Joh. 13:31**), No Respecter of Persons (**Acts 10:34**), My Witness (**Rom. 1:9**), Revealed *(the wrath of)* (**Rom. 1:18**), Manifest (**Rom. 1:19**), According to Truth (**Rom. 2:2**), Blasphemed (**Rom. 2:24**), Shed Abroad in our Hearts by the Holy Spirit (**Rom. 5:5**), Eternal Life through Jesus Christ *(the gift of)* (**Rom. 6:23**), Faithful (**1Co. 1:9; 10:13**), Wiser (**1Co. 1:25**), Stronger (**1Co. 1:25**), Not the Author of Confusion, but of Peace (**1Co. 14:33**), One (**Gal. 3:20**), Not Mocked (**Gal. 6:7**), My Record (**Php. 1:8**) *(my witness),* Not Bound *(the Word of)* (**2Ti. 2:9**), Forever and ever (**Heb. 1:8**), Quick *(Word of God)* (**Heb. 4:12**) *(Living),* Not Unrighteous (**Heb. 6:10**), Not Ashamed to be called their God (**Heb. 11:16**), Well Pleased (**Heb. 13:16**), Light (**1Jo. 1:5**), Love (**1Jo. 4:8, 16**), and With Men (**Rev. 21:3**).

"The Lord is . . ." These also are not attributes, not names, but descriptions of God, or His actions. Each are listed in order and exactly quoted, as progressively revealed about God in Scripture. These may include names or attributes. Below are over a hundred of the most meaningful, exactly quoted:

"The Lord is" In this Place (**Gen. 28:16**), Righteous (**Exo. 9:27; 2Ch. 12:6; Psa. 129:4; 145:17; Lam. 1:18**), My Strength and Song (**Exo. 15:2; Psa. 118:14**), A Man of War (**Exo. 15:3**), Become Glorious in Power *(your right hand)* (**Exo. 15:6**), Greater than all gods (**Exo. 18:11**), With us (**Num. 14:9**), Longsuffering (**Num. 14:18**), His

Inheritance (**Deu. 10:9**), Their Inheritance (**Deu. 18:2; Jos. 18:7**), Among Us (**Jos. 22:31**; cf. **Jer. 8:8**), God (**Jos. 22:34; 1Ki. 8:60; 20:28**), With You (**Jdg 6:12; 2Sa. 7:3; 2Ch. 15:2; Luk. 1:28**), Your way (**Jdg. 18:6**), A God of Knowledge (**1Sa. 2:3**), Witness (**1Sa. 12:5**), With Him (**1Sa. 16:18; 2Ki. 3:12** *(Word of)*), Departed *(from you)* (**1Sa. 28:16**), Wise (**2Sa. 14:20**), My Rock, and My Fortress, and My Deliver (**2Sa. 22:2; Psa. 16:5**), Tried (**2Sa. 22:31; Psa. 18:30**) *(trustworthy tested armor)*, The Greatness, and The Power, and The Glory, and The Victory, and The Majesty (**1Ch. 29:11**), Our God (**2Ch. 13:10**), Not With Israel (**2Ch. 25:7**), Able (**2Ch. 25:9**) *(to give you much more)*, Upon You (**2Ch. 28:11**), Your Strength (**Neh. 8:10**), Known by the Judgment *(which He executeth)* (**Psa. 9:16**), King (**Psa. 10:16**), In His Holy Temple (**Psa. 11:4**), His Refuge (**Psa. 14:6**), The Portion of Mine Inheritance and of My Cup (**Psa. 16:5**), My Rock, and My Fortress, and My Deliverer; My God, My Strength . . . My Buckler, and The Horn of My Salvation, and My High Tower (**Psa. 18:2**), Perfect (**Psa. 19:7**), Pure *(the testimony of; the commandment of)* (**Psa. 19:7 - 8**), My Shepherd (**Psa. 23:1**), With Them *(that fear Him; that uphold my soul)* (**Psa. 25:14; 54:4; Zec. 10:5**), My Light and My Salvation (**Psa. 27:1**), The Strength of My Life (**Psa. 27:1**), My Strength and My Shield (**Psa. 28:7**), Their Strength (**Psa. 28:8**), Upon the Waters . . . Upon Many Waters *(the voice of)* (**Psa. 29:3**), Powerful (**Psa. 29:4**), Full of Majesty (**Psa. 29:4**), Right *(the Word of)* (**Psa. 33:4**), Upon Them *(the eye of . . . them that fear Him)* (**Psa. 33:18**), Good (**Psa. 34:8; 100:5; 135:3; Jer. 33:11; Lam. 3:25; Nah. 1:7**), Against Them *(that do evil)* (**Psa. 34:16**; cf. **Pro. 3:33; Zep. 2:5; 1Pe. 3:12**), Near *(or nigh)* (**Psa. 34:18; 145:18; Eze. 18:25; Joel 3:14; Oba. 1:15; Zep. 1:14**), In the Heavens (**Psa. 36:5**), Among Them *(angels)* (**Psa. 68:17**), Our Defense (**Psa. 89:18**), Upright (**Psa. 92:15**), Clothed with Strength (**Psa. 93:1**), My Defense (**Psa. 94:22**), A Great God (**Psa. 95:3**). Great (**Psa. 96:4; 99:2; 135:5; Joel 2:11**), Merciful and Gracious, Slow to Anger, Plenteous in Mercy (**Psa. 103:8**), From Everlasting to Everlasting (**Psa. 103:17**), Gracious and Full of Compassion (**Psa. 111:4; 145:8**), The Beginning of Wisdom *(the fear of)* (**Psa. 111:10; Pro. 9:10**), High Above All Nations (**Psa. 113:4**), On My Side (**Psa. 118:6**), Exalted (**Psa. 118:16** *(the right hand of)*; **Isa. 33:5**), Full of Your Mercy *(the earth; "O" not "The")* (**Psa. 119:65**), Your Keeper (**Psa. 121:5**), Your Shade (**Psa. 121:5**), Round About His People (**Psa. 125:2**), Above All gods

(**Psa. 135:5**), Good to All (**Psa. 145:9**), The Beginning of Knowledge *(the fear of)* (**Pro. 1:7**), To Hate Evil *(the fear of)* (**Pro. 8:13**), Strength to the Upright *(the way of)* (**Pro. 10:29**), Strong Confidence *(the fear of)* (**Pro. 14:6**), A Fountain of Life *(the fear of)* (**Pro. 14:27**), Far from the Wicked (**Pro. 15:29**), The Instruction of Wisdom *(the fear of)* (**Pro. 15:33**), A Strong Tower *(The name of)* (**Pro. 18:10**), The Maker of Them All (**Pro. 22:2**), At Hand (**Isa. 13:6**), A God of Judgment (**Isa. 30:18**), His Treasure *(the fear of)* (**Isa. 33:6**), Our Judge (**Isa. 33:22**), Our Lawgiver (**Isa. 33:22**), Our King (**Isa. 33:22**), Well Pleased for His Righteousness' Sake (**Isa. 42:21**), Risen Upon You *(the glory of)* (**Isa. 60:1**), Not Turned Back from Us *(fierce anger)* (**Jer. 4:8**), The True God, He is the Living God (**Jer. 10:10**), With Me (**Jer. 20:11**), Gone Forth in Fury *(a whirlwind of)* (**Jer. 23:19**), His Name (**Jer. 33:2**; **Amos 5:8**; **9:6**), My Portion (**Lam. 3:24**), There (**Eze. 48:35**), His Memorial (**Hos. 12:5**), At Hand *(the day of)* (**Joel 1:15**; **Zep. 1:7**; **Php. 4:5**), Great and Very Terrible *(the day of)* (**Joel 2:11**), Slow to Anger, and Great in Power (**Nah. 1:3**), In His Holy Temple (**Hab. 2:20**), In the Midst (**Zep. 3:5, 15**) *(The Just Lord)*, My God (**Zec. 13:9**), With You (**Luk. 1:28**), Upon You (**Luk. 4:18** *(the Spirit of)*; **Acts 13:11** *(the Hand of)*), Risen (**Luk. 24:34**), One Spirit (**1Co. 6:17**), That Spirit (**2Co.. 3:17**), The Avenger (**1Th. 4:6**), Faithful (**2Th. 3:3**), My Helper (**Heb. 13:6**), Very Pitiful (**Jam. 5:11**), Gracious (**1Pe. 2:3**), Not Slack Concerning His Promise (**2Pe. 3:9**), and Salvation (**2Pe. 3:15**).

This exhaustive list didn't include the following: "His", "The Holy One", "He is . . .", "the Lord's", "God's", "of God", "of the Lord", and "God". This is the Scriptural revelation of our Great God, "the name of the Lord, the everlasting God" (**Gen. 21:31**).

God always works in perfect harmony with all of His attributes (glory, perfections, nature, character, essence, or being). He cannot work apart from them, or Himself. All of God's attributes are equal and are actively bringing to pass His sovereign plans and purposes. God is the only One completely perfect, in ANY and ALL attributes. Though His children may think they see, perceive, or feel one or more emphasized to a greater or lesser degree at times, that is merely a limited understanding of how these all work together perfectly in concert, in any given situation. Even love is seen in His holy and righteous judgment when sending someone to Hell; although, this attribute of love is usually obscured, or out of focus during judgment. Every parent understands this attribute most clearly in the discipline of a child. To love a child is to discipline, though often it is difficult and painful.

God—The Trinity

The word "Trinity" is not found in the Bible, but the truth is clearly evident throughout Scripture. The definition of the Trinity is "One God, eternally existing in three Persons (Father, Son, and Holy Spirit) No one can fully explain our unique God. Every example to describe the Trinity seems weak, at best. Three overly simplistic, though inadequate, examples are: (1) A man may be a father, son, and brother. (2) H_2O may be seen as liquid (water), solid (ice), and gas (steam). (3) The egg (shell, white, and yolk) are three distinct parts, but one egg. These simple illustrations fail as there are no parts of God, or pieces of God. The Trinity is NOT three Gods, three parts or pieces of one God, three roles or functions of one God, or three forms or modes of one God. *No one fully understands God, much less the Triune God*. *Part of our limited understanding of the Trinity is tied to our finiteness and His limitlessness in space, time, and events.*

What is the explanation and clear teaching of Scripture on the Trinity? Monotheism: There is one and only one God (**Deu. 6:4; Isa. 44:6-8; 45:5; 1Ti. 2:5; 1Co. 8:4**). All three persons of the Trinity (**Father** (**Joh 6:27; Rom. 1:7**), **Son** (**Joh. 1:1, 14; Heb. 1:8**), and **Holy Spirit** (**Acts 5:3-9**)) are Deity (God). Each is presented as equal in essence or being (**Mat. 28:19; 2Co. 13:14**). Each is presented as distinct (**Mat. 3:16 -17; Luk. 1:35; Joh. 12:28; 14:16; 15:26**). Each possesses Divine attributes and titles (as seen previously). Each accomplishes Divine works as seen below:

Divine Work	Father	Son	Holy Spirit
Creation of World	Psa. 102:25	Col. 1:16	Gen. 1:2; Job 26:13
Creation of Man	Gen. 1:27; 2:7, 22	Col. 1:16	Job 33:4
Resurrection	Act. 13:30; Rom. 6:4	Joh. 2:19; 10:17-18	Rom. 8:11
Indwelling	1Jo. 4:12, 15-16	Rom. 8:9-10	2Ti. 1:14
Sealing	Joh. 6:27	Eph. 3:17	Eph. 4:30
Miracles	Act. 2:22; 19:11	Joh. 2:11	Gal. 3:5

The Trinity is implied by the plural names and pronouns for God ("Elohim" in **Dt. 6:4**; "us" and "our" in **Gen. 1:26-27; 3:22; Isa. 6:8**) and by the Angelic proclamation, "Holy, Holy, Holy, is the LORD of hosts" (**Isa. 6:3**) and "Holy, Holy, Holy, Lord God Almighty" (**Rev. 4:8**).

Personality of God

Personality is a key aspect of personhood and central to a meaningful relationship. There are at least seven ways that God demonstrates His personhood. (1) God relates to us in a personal way and communicates to us as a person (loves, hears, grieves). (2) God possesses elements of personality, such as Intellect (**Psa. 139:1-6**), Emotions (**Nah. 1:2-3; Joh. 3:16; Eph. 4:30**), and Will (**1Th. 4:3; 5:18; 2Pe. 3:9**). (3) Two of the rational arguments (as seen above) of the anthropological or moral (man is personal and created in God's image; **Gen. 1:26**) and teleological (Design implies a Designer with similar or greater qualities) distinctly imply personhood. (4) Personal pronouns are used of God (He, Him, His, I). (5) His nature, character, attributes, or perfections (see Attributes above). (6) His names (reveals His character and naturally results in His actions or works). (7) God's proper names and characteristic names also demonstrate His unique and distinct personality and personhood.

Proper Names *(Hebrew names transliterated, if not specified)*

Elohim—"God" (Elohim, El, Elohe, or Eloah) appears 2,550 times. There are six derivatives of God listed below: (1) **El Shaddai**—"God Almighty" (**Gen. 28:3; 35:11; 43:14; 48:3; Exo. 6:3**); Greek - **Theos Pantokrator**—"God Almighty"; "Most Powerful"; "Omnipotent" (**Rev. 4:8; 11:17**). (2) **El Elyon**—"The Most High God" (**Gen. 14:18 - 20, 22; Psa. 78:56; Dan. 3:26**...); Greek - **Upsistos Theos** (**Mar. 5:7; Acts 16:17; Heb. 7:1**). (3) **El Olam**—"The Everlasting God" (**Gen. 21:33; Isa. 40:28**); Greek - **Aionios Theos** ("Everlasting," "Eternal," "without Beginning or End"; **Rev. 16:26**). (4) **El Roiy or Ra'ah**—"Thou God seest me" (**Gen. 16:13**; cf. **Isa. 58:3**); Greek - **Blepo** "You (God) seest", "discern" (**Mat. 5:31**). (5) **El Bethel**—"The God of Bethel" (**Gen. 31:13**) "House of God". (6) **El Elohe**—"The God of Israel" (**Exo. 24:10**) "God Prevails"; Greek - "Israel" "Nation of Israel"* (**Mat. 15:31**).

JEHOVAH: <u>LORD, GOD, JEHOVAH/YAHWEH</u> appears 6,519 times. There are nine derivatives of The LORD listed below. (1) **Jehovah Jireh**: "<u>The LORD will Provide</u>" (**Gen. 22:13 - 14**). (2) **Jehovah Tsaba**: "<u>The LORD of Hosts</u>" (**1Sa. 15:2; 17:45; Mal. 4:3**). (3) **Jehovah Nissi**: "<u>The LORD our Banner</u>" (**Exo. 17:8 - 15**). (4) **Jehovah M'qaddishkhem**: "<u>The LORD that Sanctifies</u>" (**Exo. 31:13; Ezra 20:12**). (5) **Jehovah Rapha or Rophe**: "<u>The LORD that Heals</u>" (**Exo. 15:26**). (6) **Jehovah Shalom**: "<u>The LORD our Peace</u>" (**Judges 6:24**). 7) **Jehovah Ra - ah**: "<u>The LORD my Shepherd</u>" (**Psa. 23:1**; cf. **80:1**). (8) **Jehovah Tsidkenu**: "<u>The LORD our Righteousness</u>" (**Jer. 23:6**). (9) **Jehovah Shammah**: "<u>The LORD is Present/There</u>" (**Eze. 48:35**).

Adonai: "<u>Lord or Master</u>" appears 431 times (Greek: <u>Kurios</u> appears 667 times). There is one derivative listed below. (1) **Adonai Yahweh**: "<u>The Lord GOD</u>" (**Gen. 15:2, 8; Isa. 41:10**)

*<u>Israel</u>—formerly named <u>Jacob the Patriarch</u>; <u>Jewish People</u>, Greek: "he shall be a prince of God"; JEHOVAH (capitalized in KJV to its "Jehovah") found 6,519 times all in the OT; "The Lord of Hosts" (226 times in Bible); many refer to "The Lord of Sabaoth" (**Rom. 9:29; James 5:4**) in the NT. Adonai is "Lord." "LORD as it appears in all uppercase letters clearly denotes the name "Jehovah."*

Characteristic Names

Some names of God that describe God or His character are: <u>Rock</u> (**Deu. 32:4, 15, 18, 30-31; 2Sa. 23:3; Psa. 18:2, 31, 46**), <u>Fortress</u> (**2Sa. 22:2; Psa. 18:2; 31:3; 91:2**), <u>Shield</u> (**Gen. 15:1; 28:7; 59:11**), <u>Mighty One</u> (**Isa. 1:24; 30:29; 49:26; 60:16** cf. **Psa. 132:2, 5**), <u>Strength</u> (**1Sa. 15:29; Exo. 15:2**), <u>Jealous</u> (**Exo. 20:5; 34:14**), <u>Judge</u> (**Gen. 18:25**), <u>Maker</u> (**Job 35:10; Isa. 54:5; Psa. 95:6**), <u>Holy One</u> (**Isa. 30:15; Psa. 71:22**), <u>Redeemer</u> (**Gen. 19:25; Isa. 48:17; 49:7, 26; 54:5, 8; 59:20**), <u>Just One</u> (**Acts 7:52; 22:14**), and <u>Everlasting Father</u> (**Mat. 6:14, 26, 32; 15:13; 18:35; Luk. 11:13**). *God is all of these, whether recognized, or not. It is awe-inspiring to meditate upon how He has been all of these characteristic names personally to His children.*

Reverence Due His Name

Rom. 2:24—"For the name of God is blasphemed among the Gentiles through you, as it is written." *Oh, may others not look at me and discount God's Might and Holiness.* **Lev. 24:16**—"And he that blasphemeth the name of the LORD, he shall surely be put to death, and all the congregation shall certainly stone him: as well the stranger, as he that is born in the land, when he blasphemeth the name of the LORD, shall be put to death." *This is serious.* **Pro. 18:10**—"The name of the LORD is a strong tower: the righteous runneth into it, and is safe."

Three of the Ten Commandments

#1—Exo. 20:3; Deu. 5:7—"Thou shalt have no other gods before Me." Hebrew: **Mynp paniym** "Before ", "**in front of**" (not letting anything cut in line; in God's rightful position). "**In my presence**" (keep them away from Me). "**In my sight**" (get them out of My face).

#2—Exo. 20:4-6; Deu. 5:8-10—"Thou shalt not make unto thee any graven image, or any likeness of anything that is in heaven above, or that is in the earth beneath, or that is in the waters beneath the earth: Thou shalt not bow down thyself unto them, nor serve them: for I the LORD thy God am a Jealous God, visiting the iniquity of the fathers upon the children unto the third and fourth generation of them that hate Me, And shewing mercy unto thousands of them that love Me and keep My commandments." No Idols (American or other); Nothing, Nowhere; For I am Jealous (for your good)—"For I the JEHOVAH, your ELOHIM am a jealous EL"; I will Judge you to great-grand Children (that Hate Me); But will give Mercy (to those who Love and Obey Me); God deserves to be #1 in our lives, because He is #1!

#3—Exo. 20:7: Deu. 5:11—"Thou shalt not take the name of the LORD thy God in vain; for the LORD will not hold him guiltless that taketh His name in vain." The use of God's name should not be disrespected (God is not "the man upstairs"; God is not the "Big daddy"); His name is not to be used flippantly ("God damn it," "Good God," or texting "OMG" for "Oh My God"). God's name is not to be used meaninglessly or carelessly ("God ___," "Jesus Christ," "Holy

___"); God's name should not be used as a <u>slang</u> or <u>substitute</u> (e.g. "Gee", "Gosh", "Golly", "Jeez", "JC"). **Eph. 4:29**—"Let no corrupt communication proceed out of your mouth, but that which is good to the use of edifying, that it may minister grace unto the hearers." **1Ti. 4:12**—"Let no man despise thy youth; but be thou an example of the believers, in word, in conversation, in charity, in spirit, in faith, in purity." **James 3:2**—"For in many things we offend all. If any man offend not in word, the same is a perfect man, and able also to bridle the whole body."

God deserves our highest respect, since the use of His name reflects our heart! Most think the "F" - word is the worse vulgarity. God says the "G" - word, when spoken in vain, meaninglessly, and carelessly, acts as if He isn't real, isn't hearing, or isn't going to judge. If using His name is NOT a prayer to Him, or a worshipful, respectful statement or Scripture about God, then IT SHOULDN'T BE SAID! Some laugh when they hear someone say, "Jesus, Mary, and Joseph"; because they think they tried to catch themselves when they started to use Jesus' name in vain as a curse word. Even pastors have heard it so commonly that from the pulpit we sometimes hear "slangs" or "substitutes." A slang for a word or name is still invoking it, whether intended or not. God deserves our utmost respect, and His name reflects our attitude and thinking. Even slang terms for Hell a literal place, is said so flippantly as "heck". Terms like "dang" are used to denote damnation. These are serious truths that shouldn't be undermined by our careless habits.

Our Response to God

After believing He is and is a rewarder of them that diligently seek Him, our response to God (all action verbs) should be: Let us Exalt, Worship, Bow Down, Kneel, Draw Near, Humble Ourselves, Bless the Lord, Rejoice in God's works, Sing unto God, Meditate Upon Him, Be glad in Him, Praise Him, Give thanks unto Him, Call upon Him, Seek His Face, Remember His marvelous works, Glory in His Holy Name— He will draw near to us and lift us up to a place we'll never want to leave or nor have to...Oh thank you heavenly Father.

Psa. 99:5—"Exalt ye the LORD our God, and worship at his footstool; for he is holy." **Psa. 95:6**—"O come, let us worship and bow down: let us kneel before the LORD our Maker." **James 4:8a**—"Draw near to God, and He will draw near to You." **James 4:10**—"Humble yourselves in the sight of the Lord and He shall lift you up." **Psa. 104:1**—"Bless the LORD, O my soul. O LORD my God, thou art very great; thou art clothed with honor and majesty." **Psa. 104:31-35**—"The glory of the LORD shall endure forever: the LORD shall rejoice in His works. He looketh on the earth, and it trembleth: he toucheth the hills, and they smoke. I will sing unto the LORD as long as I live: I will sing praise to my God while I have my being. My meditation of Him shall be sweet: I will be glad in the LORD. Let the sinners be consumed out of the earth, and let the wicked be no more. Bless thou the LORD, O my soul. Praise ye the LORD." **Psa. 105:1-5**—"O give thanks unto the LORD; call upon His name: make known His deeds among the people. Sing unto Him, sing psalms unto Him: talk ye of all His wondrous works. Glory ye in His holy name: let the heart of them rejoice that seek the LORD. Seek the LORD, and His strength: seek His face evermore. Remember His marvelous works that He hath done; His wonders, and the judgments of His mouth."

"Oh Worship The King All Glorious Above," words by Robert Grant

"O worship the King, all glorious above,
O gratefully sing His power and His love;
Our Shield and Defender, the Ancient of Days,
Pavilioned in splendor, and girded with praise.

O tell of His might, O sing of His grace,
Whose robe is the light, whose canopy space,
His chariots of wrath the deep thunderclouds form,
And dark is His path on the wings of the storm.

The earth with its store of wonders untold,
Almighty, Thy power hath founded of old;
Established it fast by a changeless decree,
And round it hath cast, like a mantle, the sea.

Thy bountiful care, what tongue can recite?
It breathes in the air, it shines in the light;
It streams from the hills, it descends to the plain,
And sweetly distills in the dew and the rain.

Frail children of dust, and feeble as frail,
In Thee do we trust, nor find Thee to fail;
Thy mercies how tender, how firm to the end,
Our Maker, Defender, Redeemer, and Friend.

O measureless might! Ineffable love!
While angels delight to worship Thee above,
The humbler creation, though feeble their lays,
With true adoration shall all sing Thy praise."

The most influential, studied, quoted, discussed person of all time; the only God-Man, Who lived, died for our sin, resurrected, lives, is coming back, and is the only way to God, His Father.

Introduction

Christology comes from the Greek stems *"Christos,"* meaning Christ, and *"logos,"* meaning a word about, the science of, or the study of; thus **Christology is the study of Jesus Christ, or God the Son**. Some key verses are **Joh. 1:1, 14** and **Col. 2:9**. **Joh. 1:1, 14** says, "In the beginning was the Word, and the Word was with God, and the Word was God. And the Word was made flesh, and dwelt among us, (and we beheld His glory, the glory as of the only begotten of the Father,) full of grace and truth." **Col. 2:9**—"For in Him dwelleth all the fullness of the Godhead bodily."

Person—Unique Above All Others

Who is Jesus Christ? How many superlative descriptions of Jesus (not necessarily names or Bible statements) can you think of that are true? Truly God is: "The Greatest", "The Most", "The Only", etc.

Greatest Teacher of All Time	*Friend*
Most Studied of All Time	**Super Star**
Most Influential Person Ever	**Master** or **Lord**
Most Talked About of All Time	**Only Messiah**
Most Quoted and Referenced Ever	**Only Always Sinless One**
Most Beloved and Hated Ever	**Only Savior** from Sin
Resurrecter from the Dead	**Only Virgin Born**
Miracle Worker	**Only Son of God**
Calendar Dates (BC and AD)	**Only God-Man**

*He resurrected Himself and told Mary that He has the power to resurrect all believers one day (**Joh. 11**). No one else has resurrected themselves, by their own power. His influence from The Sermon on the Mount, the Golden Rule, His influence on Governments is not all that He is, but His unique impression is clearly seen. He was the only*

Person born without an actual physical father. He was the only perfectly righteous man (*Isa. 9:6*). Jesus Christ has an American National Holiday celebrating His birthday, Christmas. Who is this Jesus? Josh McDowell says there are only three options: Jesus Christ is <u>Lord</u>, <u>Liar</u>, or <u>Lunatic</u>?

Person—Deity

Jesus Christ, bodily, has all the attributes of God. **Col. 2:9** says, "For in Him dwelleth all the fullness of the Godhead bodily." Mary said, "How can this be"? She believed but did not fully understand. Jesus has all the attributes of God. His attributes are identical with God, The Father. How can someone who is fully man, also have attributes which are fully God? How can this be? This question is especially asked in reference to the incommunicable attributes or those that man does not possess. God did take on human flesh. Did this lessen God? NO. Does this lessen the ability to see His divinity in all His glory? YES. The Godhead, the Trinity, the God-Man is a great miracle and mystery. This is especially difficult to understand in relationship to the three "omni" attributes. He was omniscient; yet, He grew in wisdom; He was omnipresent; yet, He limited Himself to a specific time and place in His flesh, in eternity; He was omnipotent; yet, He submitted to God, man, death, and the weaknesses of the flesh without sin). It is a reach to attempt to fully understand Christ's Deity and humanity, but consider the following. <u>For a time, Christ maintained the temporary and voluntary non-use</u> of His infinite power (example – Christ had the power to fly, but He did not use this power). In <u>"the Great Kenosis"</u> passage of Philippians 2:5-8, Christ is seen emptying, humbling and guising His glory. <u>God is not lessened</u>. However, our ability to see His Divinity and Glory is. <u>As</u> man, God took on flesh so that He would grow, learn, be in one place, be tempted, be weak, and die. <u>As God, He is</u> and <u>has all</u> the Divine attributes of God, "The Everlasting Father" (**Isa. 9:6**). <u>As the God-Man, He is God</u> in human form/man with all that is God. <u>In Jesus is</u> "ALL the fullness of the Godhead bodily" (**Col. 2:9**). Wrapped in this miraculous mystery, Jesus is a separate person in the Godhead, but truly one in His unity with God and the Holy Spirit.

Natural or Incommunicable Attributes—Deity

These are supernatural, or those that should cause worship. These attributes mankind cannot evidence. 1. Self-Existence (life)–Christ is the **Uncaused** One. He is the only completely **independent** One; He is completely **free**; 2. Pre-Existence of Jesus—Jesus existed prior to His Incarnation (Latin-"carne" - flesh), thus Christ inhabiting or taking on flesh (**Joh. 1:4; 5:26; 14:6; Col. 1:17; 1Jo. 5:20**). 3. Infinity or Infinitude—Jesus is not limited, but is bound only by His nature. His Infinity is in relationship to His Eternality—He is not limited by **time** (**Col. 1:17; 1Ti. 6:14-16; He. 1:12; Rev. 1:8; 4:8**). 4. Immensity—He is not limited by **space**, as His omnipresence is clear. **Mat. 28:20**; cf. **Col. 1:15**). Sovereignty—He is not limited by **events**, exercising total rule and control; **Col. 1:18; 1Ti. 6:15; Rev. 19:16**). 5. Spirituality (Incorporeal)—He is invisible, **without material substance** (**Col. 1:15; Joh. 4:24; Joh. 1:18**). Immutability—He is **Unchangeable** in being or essence (**Heb. 1:12; 13:8**).

Omniscience—All knowledge and understanding, including possible or actual past, present, and future. Christ has perfect knowledge, foreknowledge (**Mat. 12:25; Joh. 6:64; Luk. 5:4-8; 7:39-50; 1Co. 4:5; Col. 2:3**) with truth (**Joh. 14:6**). This is knowledge without having to discover facts since God **never learns anything**. This is knowledge that is complete and inclusive; God **always knows everything**; **Mat. 12:25**—"And Jesus knew their thoughts . . ." **Joh. 6:64**—"But there are some of you that believe not. For Jesus knew from the beginning who they were that believed not, and who should betray him."

Omnipresence—Personally **present everywhere at once** in His entirety; Christ transcends spatial limitations, which includes immensity, immanence, and transcendence (cf. **Mat. 28:20**). **Mat. 28:20**—". . . Lo, I am with you always, even unto the end of the world. Amen." This does NOT mean that parts of Him are everywhere; a material presence; Pantheistic (God is everything) or Panentheistic (God is in everything). This is difficult to understand, but Jesus existed prior to His Incarnation and now beyond His Incarnation in His human flesh! When we see Christ in heaven, we will see Him face to face. God says Christians, those that "are

46

written in <u>the Lamb's Book of Life</u>" shall see Jesus, (**Rev. 21:27**), "<u>the Lamb slain from the foundations of the world</u>" (**Rev. 13:8**), "<u>And they shall see His face…</u>" (**Rev. 22:4**). This truth caused <u>Carrie E. Breck</u> to pen the lyrics, "<u>*Face to Face*</u>". *"Face to face with Christ, my Savior, Face to face - what will it be, When with rapture I behold Him, Jesus Christ Who died for me?" **-Refrain-** "Only faintly now I see Him, With the darkened veil between, But a blessed day is coming, When His glory shall be seen." **-Refrain-** "What rejoicing in His presence, When are banished grief and pain; When the crooked ways are straightened, And the dark things shall be plain." **-Refrain-** "Face to face - oh, blissful moment! Face to face - to see and know; Face to face with my Redeemer, Jesus Christ Who loves me so."*
Refrain: *"Face to face I shall behold Him, Far beyond the starry sky; Face to face in all His glory, I shall see Him by and by!"*

<u>Omnipotence</u>: All-powerful or unlimited in power (**Rev. 1:8; Mat. 28:18; 1Ti. 6:14-16**). Jesus is Almighty, as evidenced in creation, preservation, resurrection, salvation, judgment. He is able! **Rev. 28:18**—"And Jesus came and spake unto them, saying, **All power is given unto me in heaven and in earth**." **1Ti. 6:14-16**—". . .the appearing of our **Lord Jesus Christ**: Which in His times he shall show, who is **the** blessed and **only Potentate**, the King of kings, and Lord of lords; Who only hath immortality, dwelling in the light which no man can approach unto; Whom no man hath seen, nor can see: to Whom be honor and **power everlasting**. Amen." **Rev. 1:8**—"I am Alpha and Omega, the beginning and the ending . . . **the Almighty**." *You can look at **Rev. 1:1, 5**, and **7** to clearly see it refers to Jesus if you don't recognize the "Alpha and Omega" reference. No matter what faces you, even death, Jesus is the resurrection and the life. Jesus is able, Jesus has the power you need, He has the authority. All will bow before the awesome power and rule of Jesus. Even if not here on earth as "every knee shall bow and every tongue confess"* (**Isa. 45:23; Rom. 14:11**) *"that Jesus Christ is Lord"* (**Php. 2:11**).

<u>Moral or Communicable Attributes (Personal Like God and Man)</u>
Just like God, the Father, Jesus has Moral or Communicable attributes or those that we can become like Him and His character.

47

Love: Concern, care, compassion; *Agape (see Theology Proper love attribute;* **Joh. 11:5; 13:23; 15:13, 15; 1Jo. 3:16; Rom. 8:35; 2Co. 5:14; Eph. 3:19).** **Joh. 11:5**—"Now **Jesus loved . . .**" **Joh. 13:23**—"the disciples whom **Jesus loved.**" **Joh. 15:13, 15**–"Greater love hath no man than this,** that **a man lay down his life for his friends . . . I have called you friends . . .**" **1Jo. 3:16**—"Hereby perceive we **the love of God,** because **He laid down His life for us . . .**" **Rom. 8:35a**—"Who shall separate us from the love of Christ?"** **2Cor. 5:14**—"For **the love of Christ** constraineth us . . ."** **Eph. 3:19**—"And **to know the love of Christ, which passeth knowledge, that ye might be filled with all the fullness of God."** *Jesus is the greatest expression and embodiment of love ever! (Selah).* Another attribute of His love is Mercy: Withholding of judgment, patient, long- suffering, forgiving; *not giving what is deserved* (**Heb. 2:17; Jud. 21**). **Heb. 2:17**—". . . a merciful and high priest in everything . . .**" **Jude 21**—". . . the mercy of our Lord Jesus Christ unto eternal life."** Grace: Giving of unmerited, undeserved favor; kind. *Giving what is not deserved.* "God is gracious"; "God is good"; "He gives more grace" (**Acts 15:11; Rom. 5:17, 20; 16:20, 24; 1Co. 16:23; 2Co. 8:9; 13:14; Gal. 1:6; 6:18; Php. 4:23; 1Th. 5:28; 2Th. 3:18; 1Ti. 1:14; 2Ti. 2:1; Phm. 25; Rev. 22:21**). "**The grace of Christan** (**Gal. 1:6**), "the grace that is in **Christ Jesus**" (**2Ti. 2:1**), "the grace of the Lord Jesus Christ" (**Acts 15:11; 2Co. 13:14**), "the grace of our Lord" (**1Ti. 1:14**), and "the grace of our Lord Jesus Christ" (**Rom. 16:20, 24; 1Co. 16:23; 2Co. 8:9; Gal. 6:18; Php. 4:23; 1Th. 5:28; 2Th. 3:18; Phm. 25; Rev. 22:21**). **Rom. 5:17, 20**—"For if by one man's offence death reigned by one; much more they which **receive abundance of grace** and of **the gift** of righteousness shall reign in life **by one, Jesus Christ**). Moreover the law entered, that **the offence might abound.** But where sin abounded, **grace did much more abound**". **2Co. 8:9**—"For **ye know the grace of our Lord Jesus Christ, that, though He was rich, yet for your sakes He became poor, that ye through His poverty might be rich."**

Holiness—absolute perfection; separate from sin or evil (**Heb. 4:15; 7:26; Acts 3:14; Rom. 1:4; cf. Isa. 6:3; Rev. 4:8**). Another related attribute of holiness is righteousness. Righteousness: God's standard of perfection (His Person and Law); "**the righteousness of God and our Savior Jesus Christ**" and "**Jesus Christ the righteous**" (**2Pe. 1:1; Rom. 5:18; 1Jo. 2:1**). *Righteous is not just the absence of sin, it is the presence of perfection. Sin is anything less than 0 down to 100% sinfulness or evil. Righteousness is anything greater than 0 up to 100%. Righteousness is as far above 0 as Sin is below it. God's holiness or righteousness is always perfect (100%+). Christians have been given the righteousness of Christ, when we could not attain it ourselves!* Justice is also related to holiness. <u>Justice</u>—fairness; not violating Christ's righteousness, but implementing it; "**His Son Jesus . . . the Holy One and Just**" (**Acts 3:13 - 14; 7:52; 22:14**); moral equality—"**God is no respecter of persons**" (**Deu. 32:4; Acts 10:34; 2Ch. 19:7; Rom. 2:11; Eph. 6:9; 1Pe. 1:17**; Jesus—**Joh. 12:32**).

<u>Unity</u>—One God (**Joh. 10:30; 17:22; 1Co. 8:6; 12:12; Eph. 4:5; 1Jo. 5:7**). <u>Truth</u>—perfect alignment with reality; no error, deception, or lie. In His unity he is fact, fidelity, faithful, consistent, constant, reliable (**Joh. 1:14, 17; 14:6; Heb. 6:18**); Jesus is "full of grace and truth"; **Faithful**—adheres to promises; steadfast to standard, to truth, in affection; loyal (Hebrew - **Checed, hesed** - loyal love, mercies; gives strong assurance—**Rom. 8:38-39**).

<u>Scripture on Christ's Deity</u>

Joh. 8:58—"Before Abraham was, <u>I AM</u>" (cf. **Exo. 3:14; Isa. 43:13**). *(Before birth, Jesus "is"; eternal).* **Mic. 5:2**—". . . <u>Whose goings forth have been from of old, from everlasting</u>"*(eternal).* **Col. 2:9**—"For <u>in Him dwelleth all the fullness of the Godhead bodily.</u>" *(Jesus is completely God).* **Joh. 1:1-4, 14**—"In the beginning was the Word, and the Word was with God, and <u>the Word was God</u>. The same was in the beginning with God. <u>All things were made by Him</u>; and <u>without Him was not anything made that was made</u>. <u>In Him was life</u>; and the life was the light of men... And the Word was made flesh, and dwelt among us, (and we beheld His glory, the glory as of the only begotten of the Father,) full of grace and truth." *(Jesus was God and with God; in the beginning, Jesus created all).* **Mat. 1:23**— "Behold, a virgin shall be with child, and shall bring forth <u>a Son</u>, and they shall call His name <u>Emmanuel, which being interpreted is, God</u>

with us" (Isa. 7:14). *(Jesus is God with us).* **Isa. 9:6**—"For unto us <u>a</u> <u>Child is born</u>, unto us <u>a Son</u> is given: and the government shall be upon His shoulder: and <u>His name shall be called</u> Wonderful, Counselor, <u>The Mighty God</u>, <u>The Everlasting Father</u>, The Prince of Peace." *(Jesus called The Mighty God, The Everlasting Father).* **Joh. 3:31**—"He that cometh from above <u>is above all</u>: he that is of the earth is earthly, and speaketh of the earth: <u>He that cometh from</u> <u>heaven is above all.</u>" **Joh. 8:23**—"And He said unto them, Ye are from beneath; <u>I am from above</u>: ye are of this world; I am not of this world." *(Jesus came from heaven; men from earth).* **Joh. 10:30**—"<u>I</u> <u>and my Father are one.</u>" *(God the Father and Son are one God).* **Joh. 13:3**—"Jesus knowing that <u>the Father had given all things into His</u> <u>hands</u>, and that <u>He was come from God, and went to God.</u>" *(Omniscience).* **Joh. 17:5**—"And now, O Father, <u>glorify Thou Me with</u> <u>Thine own Self</u> with <u>the glory which I had with Thee</u> <u>before the world</u> <u>was.</u>" *(Jesus had glory before He was born; the same glory as God the Father).* **1Ti. 3:16**—"And without controversy great is the mystery of godliness: <u>God was manifest in the flesh</u>, justified in the Spirit, seen of angels, preached unto the Gentiles, believed on in the world, received up into glory." *(Jesus is God in the flesh).* **Heb. 13:8**—"<u>Jesus Christ</u> <u>the same</u> <u>yesterday</u>, and <u>today</u>, and <u>forever.</u>" *(Jesus is immutable).* **Rev. 1:8, 11**—"I am <u>Alpha and Omega</u>, <u>the</u> <u>beginning and the ending</u>, saith <u>the Lord</u>, which is, and which was, and which is to come, <u>the Almighty.</u> Saying, I am <u>Alpha and Omega</u>, <u>the first and the last</u> . . ." *(Jesus the beginning/first and ending/last; also the All Powerful).* **Heb. 1:2-8**—"Hath in these last days spoken unto us by <u>His Son</u>, whom He hath appointed <u>heir of all things</u>, by Whom also <u>He made the worlds</u>; Who being <u>the brightness of His</u> <u>glory</u>, and <u>the express image of His person</u>, and <u>upholding all things</u> <u>by the word of His power</u>, when He had by <u>Himself purged our sins</u>, sat down on the right hand of the Majesty on high; Being made <u>so</u> <u>much better than the angels</u>, as He hath by inheritance obtained <u>a</u> <u>more excellent name than they.</u> For unto which of the angels said he at any time, Thou art <u>My Son</u>, this day have I begotten thee? And again, I will be to him a Father, and He shall be to me a Son? And again, when He bringeth in the Firstbegotten into the world, He saith, And let all the angels of God <u>worship Him.</u> And of the angels he saith, <u>Who maketh His angels</u> spirits, and His ministers a flame of fire. But <u>unto the Son</u> He saith, <u>Thy throne, O God</u>, is for ever and ever: a scepter of righteousness is the scepter of Thy kingdom. And, Thou, Lord, in the beginning hast laid the foundation of the earth; and <u>the heavens are the works of Thine hands</u>." *(Jesus created all; the express image of God; holds everything together by His own power; cleansed our sin; created angels and is so much better than angels; is to be worshipped; God the Father calls Him God. The Hebrew and Greek word for angel means "messenger, angel, ambassador, or king." For those who say Jesus is only an angel, Satan's brother, or other non-Biblical nonsense, God says in Hebrews 1 that Jesus: (1) "Created the angels," (2) "Is So much better than the angels," (3) Has "a more excellent name than" the angels, and (4) "Let all the angels of God worship Him;" Jesus is the greatest messenger and revealer of God).*

"Theophany or <u>Christophany</u>"

"The Angel of Jehovah," not "an angel" frequently is believed to be the pre-Incarnate Christ. Some believe that was an exception name, and only an angel. Most believe this was Jesus (prior to His taking on permanent flesh) coming as a messenger of God to man and even disguising Himself as a man, as did other angels (cf. **Gen. 16:7-13; 22:11-18**). Several examples of this are found in Genesis and Joshua where the "Angel of God" is called God. **Gen. 22:15-16**—"And **the Angel of the LORD** called unto Abraham out of heaven the second time, And said, **By Myself have I sworn, saith the LORD** . . ." **Gen. 31:11-13**—"And **the Angel of God** spake . . . I am the God of Bethel** . . ." Many refer to these appearances as a Theophany or a Christophany (Greek *"Theos"*—God; *"Christos"*—Christ and *"phaino"*—to appear) or appearances of God (**Gen. 18:1- 33; Jos. 5:13-15**). In **Gen. 18:1 - 33** (**"The LORD"** and two Angels that **appeared like "three men"**); **Jos. 5:13-15** (**"Captain of the LORD'S host" appeared like "a man"**).

Virgin Birth Demonstrates Deity

The Virgin Birth is demonstrated in Scripture (**Mic. 5:2; Mat. 2:1**). **Gen. 3:15**—"her seed" (women don't have seed), "His heel" (Christ's on the cross). **Isa. 7:14**—"the Lord Himself," "<u>virgin shall conceive</u>," "bear a Son" (virgin birth), "His name Immanuel." **Mat. 1:18**— "<u>before they came together</u>, she was found with child of the Holy Spirit." **Mat. 1:20**—"<u>that which is conceived in her is of the Holy Spirit</u>." **Mat. 1:23**—"Behold, <u>a virgin shall be with child</u>, and shall bring forth a Son, and they shall call His name Emmanuel, which being interpreted is, God with us." **Mat. 1:25**—"And <u>knew her not till she had brought forth her firstborn Son</u>: and he called his name JESUS" ("knew her not," "knew" used as a euphemism for "sexual intimacy"). **Luk. 1:27**—"<u>virgin espoused to a man</u>," "<u>the virgin's</u> name was Mary" (Mary was a virgin). **Luk. 1:34-35**—"Then said Mary unto the angel, '<u>How shall this be, seeing I know not a man</u>?' And the angel answered and said unto her, 'The <u>Holy Spirit shall come upon thee</u>, and <u>the power of the Highest shall overshadow thee</u>: therefore also <u>That holy thing which shall be born of thee shall be called the Son of God</u>.'" ("Know" again for "sex"; Holy Spirit responsible for "her seed"). *There are many incredible reasons for the Virgin Birth (besides His Deity—in order to be fully God and man) when we get to anthropology (man) and Hamartiology (sin) and how sin is passed down from generation to generation under the depravity of man.*

Sinlessness Demonstrates Deity

The Bible says Jesus was sinless His entire life. Jesus is the only sinless person ever. Some believe Mary was also sinless, although the Bible says that "all have sinned" (**Rom. 3:23**) and all are sinners (**1Ki. 8:46; 2Ch. 6:36; Psa. 14:3; 53:3; Ecc. 7:20; Rom. 3:10-19; Gal. 3:22**; etc. (*see Hamartiology*). Jesus is the sinless One. Only Jesus lived a perfect life. **Heb. 4:15**–Jesus ". . . was in all points tempted like as we are, yet <u>without sin</u>." **2Co. 5:21**—"For He hath made Him to be sin for us, <u>Who knew no sin</u>; that we might be made the righteousness of God in Him." **1Pe. 2:22**—"Who <u>did no sin</u>, neither was guile found in His mouth." **1Jo. 3:5**—"And ye know that He was manifested to take away our sins; and <u>in Him is no sin</u>." *There are two views on how Jesus was/is sinless. He's is impeccable. He is, was, and always will be God and all that it entails:*

Peccability–This view purports that Jesus was capable of sinning, but didn't. Peccability maintains that Christ's temptation was not and could not be real, if Jesus could not really fail that temptation. Those who hold this view assert that God cannot be tempted with evil as it says in **James 1:12-15**, but this doesn't account for the fact that the Bible says in **Heb. 4:15**, Jesus ". . . was in all points tempted like as we are, yet without sin."

Impeccability—This view holds that Jesus was incapable of sinning, and did not sin. The temptation was real, even though Jesus was sure to always perfectly overcome it; He did not yield to the temptation.   The Scripture is clear that God cannot be tempted. God wasn't tempted, the God-man was indeed tempted; so, <u>what happened during His temptations</u>, or how was He tempted? His humanity was tempted, which was inseparable from His Deity. Though earthly examples are trite when attempting to explain the heavenly truths, sometimes word pictures are helpful (e.g. A small piece of pliable wire can be bent. If this same small wire were welded to a railroad beam the railroad beam could not be bent. The two could not be separated, thus guaranteeing no bending of either of them since welded together). Since Jesus is incapable of sinning now (cf. **Heb. 1:12**), He couldn't have sinned then (cf. **He. 13:8**). He had no sin nature as the 2nd Adam (**Rom. 5:12; 1Co. 15:22, 45-49**). Was the <u>temptation real</u>, or if He couldn't sin, was it a real temptation? *Yes! In His humanity He chose to submit to the will of the Father; moreover, as God, He was certain to do so. It does not make a test any less real if you make a perfect score on it. This is similar to the offer of salvation to the non-elect or the offer of the Kingdom during the 1st Advent. These were legitimate offers, even though God knew they would be rejected. It was a legitimate temptation, although God knew He wouldn't and couldn't sin and would always be perfect. Jesus measured up to His Law, His person, and His standard of perfection. The test was based on His abilities, so naturally and supernaturally He would always pass any test.*

Why is this so important? <u>What's at stake</u>? <u>Christ's Deity is at stake</u>; if He could have sinned, He wasn't truly God. <u>God's Word is at stake</u>;

if He wasn't tempted, God is a liar. <u>Christ's Mediation is at stake</u>; if He didn't feel our weaknesses, He couldn't truly understand. He is our faithful High Priest and Mediator. *The most important truth is that He was tempted, but did NOT sin. The Law is a reflection of God's nature, Who He is. The Law expresses the character of God. Certainly, Jesus (who is God), couldn't behave differently than His nature allowed. Jesus did NOT have a sin nature. He possessed the nature of God and the sinless nature of man in one. Jesus did not have the sin nature, like all men after Adam. He was like Adam before the Fall; yet Jesus didn't fall. This is also important as Jesus shows us how to have victory over sin, when tempted (cf. **Luke 4**, He quoted Scripture). This discussion will be addressed in the Doctrine of Sin, or Hamartiology.*

The Trinity—Member of the One Godhead

The Trinity (see Theology Proper) includes Jesus Christ as the 2nd member or Person of the Godhead. You see this about Christ in the **OT** by: 1) Plural names, e.g. "Elohim" (**Deu. 6:4**), 2) Plural personal pronouns—"us" "our" (**Gen. 1:26 - 27; 11:7; Isa. 6:8**), and 3) Theophanes, Christophanes, or the Angel of the Lord (**Gen. 18:1f; 22:15-16; 31:11-13; Jos. 5:13-15**). You see Christ as a member of the Trinity in the **NT** by: (1) <u>Christ's baptism</u> (**Mat. 3:16-17**), which was like no other, with visible involvement by the other two members of the Trinity (His Father and the Holy Spirit), (2) <u>Believer's baptism</u> (**Mat. 28:19**) " . . . baptizing them in the name of the Father, and of the Son, and of the Holy Ghost" (which implies equality), (3) <u>Paul's benediction</u> (**2Co. 13:14**), "The grace of the Lord Jesus Christ, and the love of God, and the communion of the Holy Ghost, *be* with you all. Amen." (Implied equality), and (4) <u>The Father is God</u> (**Rom. 1:7; Joh. 1:18**), <u>Christ is God</u> (**Heb. 1:8; Joh. 1:1-18**), and <u>the Holy Spirit is God</u> (**Act. 5:3-4; 1Co. 2:9-10**).

Titles and Names of God

Some of the titles of Jesus and names that reflect His Deity are: <u>Son of God</u> (**Ps. 2:7**), <u>First Begotten</u> (Greek "prototokos") (**Mat. 1:25; Luk. 2:7; Rom. 8:29; Col. 1:15, 18; Heb. 1:6; Rev. 1:5**), <u>Only Begotten</u> (Greek "monogenes") (**Joh. 1:14, 18; 3:16, 18; 1Jo. 4:9**), <u>Jehovah</u>

(**Zec. 2:10; Jer. 23:5-6**), Elohim (Greek "theos" —God) (**Isa. 9:6**), Adonai (Greek "kurios" —Lord) (**Psa. 110:1**), Holy One of God (**Luk. 4:34**), Savior (**Luk. 1:47; 2:11**), Jesus (**Mat. 1:16, 18**), Christ the Lord (**Luk. 2:11**), Immanuel—"God with us" (**Isa. 7:14; Mat. 1:23**), Lamb of God (**Joh. 1:29**), Master (**Luk. 17:13**), The Resurrection and the Life (**Joh. 11:25**), The Lord of Righteousness (**Jer. 23:16**), God (**1Jo. 5:20; Joh. 1:1, 14; Heb. 1:8**), Son (**Heb. 1:8; Isa. 9:6**), Wonderful (**Isa. 9:6**), Counselor (**Isa. 9:6**), Mighty God (**Isa. 9:6**), Everlasting Father (**Isa. 9:6**), Prince of Peace (**Isa. 9:6**), Messiah (**Dan. 9:25 - 26**), Christ (**Mat. 1:16, 18**), King of Kings (**Rev. 19:16**), Lord of Lords (**Rev. 19:16**), The Word of God (**Joh. 1:1, 14; Rev. 19:13**), Faithful and True (**Rev. 19:11**), Alpha and Omega (**Rev. 1:8, 11, 17-18; 21:6; 22:13**), Bright and Morning Star (**Rev. 22:16**), and I AM (**Joh. 8:58**).

Person—Humanity

Humanity is indicated by having **human parents** (**Mat. 1:28; 2:11; 12:47; Luk. 2:41, 43, 48; Joh. 1:14; 2:1; Acts 13:23; Rom. 1:3; Gal. 4:4; Gen. 3:13**f). There are many OT prophesies of the Messiah's lineage. Jesus had human siblings (brothers and sisters) (**Mat. 13:55-56; Mar. 6:3**). Christ had human physical and mental growth (**Luk. 2:40, 52**). Jesus had human titles and names like: "the Son of man" (**Mat. 9:6; 12:8**...), "the Son of Adam" and "the last Adam" (**Luk. 3:38; 1Co. 15:45**), "the Son of Abraham" (**Mat. 1:1; Luk. 3:34**), "the Son of David" (**Mat. 1:1; 21:9**), "of the tribe of Judah" (**Rev. 5:5**), "Jesus of Nazareth" (**Mar. 1:24; 10:47**), "the King of the Jews" (**Mat. 27:37**), "Good Shepherd" (**Joh. 10:11, 14**), and "High Priest" (**Heb. 9:11**).

His humanity is indicated by His **human characteristics** with a body (**Mat. 26:12; Heb. 2:14**) that was: circumcised (**Luk. 2:21**), baptized (**Luk. 3:21**), hungry (**Mat. 4:2**), thirsty (**Joh. 19:28**), weary (**Joh. 4:6**), agony and sweat (**Luk. 22:44**), grew (**Luk. 2:40, 52**), and died (**Mat. 4:2; Luk. 2:40; 22:44; Joh. 4:5-6, 19:28**). His humanity is indicated by His **human parts** (flesh, blood, bones, hands, feet, side, voice, brow, head, etc.). *For the life of the flesh is in the blood . . .*" (***Lev. 17:11***), "*. . . without shedding of blood, there is no forgiveness.*" (***Heb. 9:22***), "*. . . made them white in the blood of the Lamb*" (***Rev. 17:14***). *He had to take on flesh and have blood to die, to forgive, and to make* *clean.* Jesus also had a <u>soul</u> (**Mat. 26:38; Mar. 14:34; Joh. 12:27**), which included emotions. He was <u>angry</u> (**Mar. 11:15 - 18**), He <u>cried</u> (**Joh. 11:35**), Jesus learned or "<u>grew in wisdom</u>" (**Luk. 2:52**), and experienced man's feelings and weaknesses (**Heb. 4:15**). Jesus also had a <u>Spirit</u> (**Luk. 23:46**), which <u>passed through walls</u> (**Luk. 24:36-37**) and <u>walked on water</u> (**Mat. 14:25-26; Mar. 6:48-49**).

The Bible called Jesus human, or a man (**1Ti. 2:5; Rom. 5:15**). **1Ti. 2:5**—"For there is one God, and one Mediator between God and men, the man Christ Jesus." **Rom. 5:15**—"But not as the offence, So also is the free gift. For if through the offence of one many be dead, much more the grace of God, and the gift by grace, which is by one man, Jesus Christ, hath abounded unto many." *He was fully man since the Incarnation. What love that God would confine Himself to the frailty of our flesh forever to save us.* **Heb. 2:14, 17**—*"Forasmuch then as the children are partakers of <u>flesh and blood</u>, He also Himself likewise <u>took part of the same</u>...Wherefore <u>in all things</u> it behoved Him <u>to be made like unto His brethren</u> . . ."* Why? **Heb. 2:14, 17**—*"that <u>through death</u> He might <u>destroy</u> him that had the power of <u>death</u>, that is, the <u>devil</u> . . . to <u>make reconciliation</u> for the sins of the people."* The spiritual battle with flesh and blood could only be won by flesh and blood, by Jesus Christ as our Divine Substitute.*

Deity and Humanity in One Forever

Deity and humanity are united in one forever (**Joh. 1:1-14; Rom. 1:2-5; 1Ti. 3:16; Heb. 2:14; 1Jo. 1:1-3**). The 2nd member of the Godhead became the God-Man. This is what theologians call the hypostatic union—the union of 100% God and 100% man. This happened at the Incarnation of Christ; Deity taking on humanity and veiling His Deity, sometimes referred to as the great "Kenosis," or emptying (cf. **Php. 2:5-11**). <u>What happened to His attributes</u>? Temporary and voluntary nonuse of certain attributes, a veiling of His person and glory. He still possessed attributes, but they were not necessarily active. I can see, but may choose not to. <u>Who died</u>, God or Man, or God and Man? The God-Man. <u>How is the Deity and Humanity in Christ different than God indwelling Christians (any other human indwelt by Deity)</u>? Jesus is the only fully God and fully human person ever, and was such at conception. A believer at salvation, is indwelt by the Holy Spirit, and as such, may be conformed to the image of God more fully and powerfully, but is not God, but a man—because God chooses to live in them to the extent they yield to Him. It is God living in them, not that they are or become God. The one Mediator between God and Man (**1 Timothy 2:5** says, "For *there is* one God, and one Mediator between God and men, the man Christ Jesus"). A Mediator must be representative of both parties. Jesus couldn't have accomplished that mediation if He weren't both God and man.

Christ's Work

As a result of His works, Jesus deserves and received worship (**Mat. 2:11; 8:2; 9:18; 14:33; 15:25; 28:9, 17; Mar. 5:6; Luk. 24:52; Joh. 9:38; Rev. 5:14**). The Bible says, Jesus <u>created and preserves the universe</u> (**Col. 1:15-18; Joh. 1:1, 14**). Jesus did many <u>supernatural miracles</u>: over nature (**Mat. 4:18-22; Mar. 1:16-20; Luk. 5:1-11**), over sickness and disease (**Mat. 12:9-21; Joh. 5:1-47**), over Satan and his demons (**Mar. 1:21-28; Luk. 4**), over sin to forgive (**Mat. 9:1-8; Mar. 2:1-12; Luk. 5:17-26**), over man's greatest enemy, death (**Mat. 9:18-26; Mar. 5:21-43**), and many miraculous works (**Mat. 11:4-5, 21, 23; Mar. 6:2; Joh. 2:11, 23; 3:2; 6:2; 7:31; 9:16; 11:47; 12:37; Acts 2:22**). Jesus <u>taught</u> (**Mar. 5:35**) and <u>preached</u> (**Mar. 1:38**). Jesus primarily came to earth to die for sinners so man could be saved (**1Ti. 2:15**).

The death and burial of Jesus was a **Substitutionary Atonement**. Christ died in our place (**2Co. 5:21; 1Pe. 2:24; 3:18; Isa. 53:6**). Adam (1st) <u>represented us in sin</u>; Christ (2nd Adam) <u>represented us in salvation</u> (**Rom. 5:12-21; 1 Co. 15:22**). Both representations are appropriated by our choice. *All believe the choice was God's election or predestination. Man has free will to choose as do those who maintain "<u>Conditional Election</u>"* and "<u>Unlimited Atonement</u>"* (see both below). The view of substitutionary atonement is tied directly to a person's view of election. Jesus paid the complete penalty for our sin by His Death and Burial. He took our place in the judgment we deserved. It is the OT picture of the scapegoat (**Lev. 16**). One goat was chosen and sacrificed; the other was released alive as the Scapegoat. Jesus was chosen by God to die in our place; hence, we* *are released free and alive, as the scapegoat pictured. Atonement was made by someone else (Jesus) to God for someone else (man). Jesus is our sacrifice; we are the metaphorical scapegoat.*

Many theological works discuss election and grace under Theology Proper since God Elected by Grace. Those discussions usually follow and discuss atonement under Christology as Christ's blood atones. However, here is a brief summarization of both primary views together. Since Jesus is God, the entire Godhead was involved, and these are tightly related in the understanding of these deep doctrines of our glorious God. Also these three are the middle three of the five letter Calvinistic acrostic, **TULIP** (**T**otal Depravity - discussed in Hamartiology, **U**nconditional Election, **L**imited Atonement, **I**rresistible Grace, and **P**erseverance of the Saints - discussed in Soteriology). These represent such a strong debate by Christians across denominations between Calvinists (frequently Reformed, Christian Reformed, and Presbyterians as seen in the Westminster Confession) and Arminians (Methodists, et. al.) as seen in the Seven Tenets of Arminianism or Five Articles of Remonstrance.

For whom is Christ's death, burial, and resurrection? Who may be saved? **Unconditional Election** is the belief that God's election of some men to eternal salvation is based on nothing, except God's will alone. In contrast, **Conditional Election*** is God's election, or predestination of some men to eternal salvation based on His foreknowledge (omniscience, knowing beforehand) of man's response to God's offer and work (**Rom. 8:29; 1Pe. 1:2**). Literally, there are hundreds of verses with the "condition of faith" to be saved (e.g. **Joh. 1:12; 3:16, 18; 6:47; Acts 16:31**); for God to be fair/just (all given a chance; **Deu. 32:4; 2Sa. 23:3; Job 4:17; Psa. 7:9; Pro. 16:11**); for God not to be capricious/arbitrary/partial (God is no "respecter of persons"; **2Ch. 19:7; Mat. 5:45; Acts 10:34; Rom. 2:11; Eph. 6:9; 1Pe. 1:17**); for God to be good (**Exo. 34:6; Psa. 27:13; 31:19; 33:5; 52:1; 145:7; Rom. 2:4; Gal. 5:22**); for God to hold man responsible or accountable (would make God the author of sin and not man); for man not to be a robot (man has free will to choose, obey, or disobey; **Deu. 30:19; Jos. 24:15; Pro. 3:31**); God is not willing that any should perish; therefore, He could NOT "will" most to perish forever; **2Pe. 3:9)**. The discussion that follows the unconditional and conditional election beliefs is **Single** versus **Double Predestination** or **Election** (In single election God unconditionally elects only the saved: He doesn't elect the unsaved. In double predestination, or election God elects a small few to heaven and elects the majority to Hell). *Many people believe in Single claiming God only elected to salvation, but not to damnation. However, that weakens and undermines God's Sovereignty. God completely and totally elects all that has been, is, or will be. So, whom does God choose?—All who believe/receive.*

What is the extent of His Substitutionary Atonement, which is so closely connected to election, or the application of His death and burial? In the **Limited Atonement** view Christ died only for the small number of elect, not the majority or reprobate versus **Unlimited Atonement*** in which Christ died for all sin and sinners and offers atonement to all (elect and non-elect). Christ's righteousness, perfection, and blood were more than sufficient! Those viewing Christ's death as providing unlimited atonement take the Bible literally. The Bible says "all" and "all" means "all". Not all, or everyone, will be saved, clearly as only those who accept God's gift or appropriate Christ's death by "faith" will be saved. The Limited Atonement position asserts that if Christ died for all, then all will be saved or **Universalism**. *Since rejecting God's gift and pardon will not force you into God's home, and there is only one unpardonable sin (rejecting Him and His pardon), why does a person go to Hell? Most would just respond that a person's sin sends them to Hell; but what sin? Sin is rejecting God and His Gift (Blasphemy of the Holy Spirit— see Pneumatology). For what sin(s) does Christ death pay?—ALL.*

I hold the unlimited atonement view for the following reasons: <u>God and man's character require and prove it.</u> <u>God is Holy and Omnipresent</u>, and He must cleanse the universe of all sin; even Satan's and his demons—**Lev. 11:44 - 45; 19:2; 1Ch. 16:29; Isa. 6:3; 1Pe. 1:16; Rev. 4:8; Psa. 19:7; Mat. 5:48; Jam. 1:13**. *All sin had to be paid for completely, but some sinners will reject His Atonement and* *receive judgment. Even the sin of Satan and his demons had to be paid, though obviously God did not take on the "flesh" or nature of angels or even offer them salvation (cf. **Heb. 2:16**). Incidentally, the fallen angels were in the very presence of God and chose to reject Him and a relationship with Him. Christ offers this atonement (salvation) to all men, yet some blaspheme the Spirit's miraculous drawing of them to Christ, and rightly will not be forgiven. These blaspheming people will receive judgment in Hell with Satan and his demons because of their rejection of what Jesus has already accomplished for them. Christ's shed blood was not only sufficient to cleanse all the sin in the universe (including the non-elect man and angels), but necessary. All sin has been paid for by Christ's death providing atonement. In a moment of time, the eternal, infinite, perfect God paid for all sin (past, present, and future). The penalty is removed only for the elect or those not rejecting, but appropriating the grace of Atonement by faith.*

God is Fair and Just and all given a chance for salvation; **Deu. 32:4; 2Sa. 23:3; Job 4:17; Psa. 7:9; Pro. 16:11**). God is Good and Loving (**Exo. 34:6; Psa. 27:13; 31:19; 33:5; 52:1; 145:7; Rom. 2:4; Joh. 3:16; 1Jo. 4:8, 16**). God is not Capricious and Arbitrary; God is no "respecter of persons"; **2Ch. 19:7; Mat. 5:45; Acts 10:34; Rom. 2:11; Eph. 6:9; 1Pe. 1:17**). Man is Responsible and Accountable (would make God the author of sin not man)"Therefore, choose life" (**Deu. 30:19; Gal. 3:6; Mat. 12:36; 18:23; Rom. 14:12; 1Pe. 4:5**). Man has Free Will; man is not a robot; man has free will to choose, obey, or sin; **Joh. 8:36; 1Co. 9:19; Deu. 30:19; Jos. 24:15; 1Ch. 21:10f; Pro. 1:29; 3:31; Isa. 7:14 - 15; 56:4; 65:12**). *Imputation of sin (Hamartiology) will be discussed in greater detail in a subsequent section. If God created man to sin, forces him to Hell when he does, then this makes God responsible for man's sin. This takes a harsh view of God if He created man to sin without providing a way to be saved from it.*

I hold the unlimited view of atonement because God "is not willing that any should perish, but that all should come to repentance" (**2Pe. 3:9**). If limited atonement were true, His will would have been for most to perish, and perish forever, without a chance. The main reason is I hold the unlimited view is <u>God's Word requires and proves it</u> (**Joh. 1:29; Rom. 5; 11:32; 2Co. 5:14-15, 19; 2Pe. 2:1; 3:9; 1Jo. 4:14;** plus the following quotes). **Jn. 12:32**—"And <u>I</u>, if I be lifted up from the earth, <u>will draw **all men** unto me</u>." **Col. 1:20**—"And, <u>having made peace through the blood of His cross</u>, by Him <u>to reconcile **all things** unto Himself;</u> by Him, I say, <u>whether they be things in earth, or things in heaven</u>." **1Ti. 2:4, 6**—"Who will have **all men** <u>to be saved</u>, and to come unto the knowledge of the truth. Who gave Himself a ransom **for all**, to be testified in due time." **1Ti. 4:10**—". . . Who **is the Savior of all men**, specially of those that believe." **Tit. 2:11**—"For the grace of God that <u>bringeth salvation hath appeared</u> **to all men**." **Heb. 2:9**—"that <u>He</u> by the grace of God <u>should taste death for every man</u>." **1Jo. 2:2**—"And He is <u>the propitiation for our sins</u>: and **not for ours only**, but also **for the sins of the whole world**." *Although there are many studied theologians and people who hold a limited view of atonement, I believe that we should allow Scripture to define our views, and when we do, it leads all to an Unlimited Atonement view. ALL and EVERY mean ALL and EVERY (elect and non-elect). It doesn't mean only a small percentage of men (only the elect). 1Jn. 2:2 could not be any clearer for those who want to change the meaning of "all" to mean only all the elect. God even contrasts His propitiation or satisfaction of sins, not just with the elect or us saved (our), but "not for ours only", "but also for the sins of the whole world." Numerous other verses exist. So rest; God is satisfied with the death and payment by His Son! In addition,* <u>evangelistic motivation and zeal require all to be able to be saved</u>. If a person believes God is cruel and elects, or has only paid for the sin of elect individuals, then there is no motivation to witness. Since it is impossible to know who the elect are, and the elect will be saved anyway, why does God tell us to "go into all the world and preach the gospel (Mt. 18:19-20)?

Who receives and how do they receive God's grace? **Irresistible Grace**, or **Efficacious Grace** is the view that maintains that God's grace can NOT be resisted, and only the elect will be saved; This view presupposes that God, (by giving knowledge and working of the Holy

Spirit in a way He does NOT with the non-elect) causes elect men to choose Him and they can NOT do otherwise). This view is in opposition to a **Prevenient Grace** view in which God gives grace to ALL and draws ALL (elect and reprobate) by His Holy Spirit. Those who receive Christ by faith are elected and saved. Likewise, those who resist, reject, or blaspheme the Holy Spirit's miraculous work of enlightenment and drawing are reprobate because they reject God's gift of eternal salvation. Someone once wisely said, "Without God, we cannot; without man, God will not." God's Spirit "prevents" from continuing in sin and "precedes" any action or ability of anyone, convicts of sin (**Joh. 16:8, 13**), graciously enlightens and draws all the spiritually dead who are in sin (**Tit. 2:11**; **Eph. 2:1**; **Col. 2:13**) by the Word of the truth of the gospel (**Joh. 12:32**; **Eph. 1:17-20**), prompting a spiritual desire and understanding to return to God. Received grace, by faith, results in salvation (**Eph. 2:8-9**), while resisted or rejected grace results in blindness, blasphemy, and death (**Mat. 12:31-32**; **Mar. 3:28 - 29**; **Luk. 12:10**; **Joh. 12:48**; **Rom. 13:2**). The unsaved resist God's Spirit (**Acts 7:51**; **2Ki. 17:13-15**) and the saved resist and grieve God's Spirit every time they sin (**Eph. 4:30**). God does NOT force Himself on anyone for salvation; that would be paramount to spiritual rape (cf. **Rev. 3:20** where God doesn't use forcible entry). *Prevenient grace maintains restoration of enough original capacity to respond to God's grace. Does God permit man to resist Him, or is He irresistible? Does man have free will, and does God enable him to choose Him? For how many sins does God say He died and draws? To how many does God offer salvation and command us to evangelize? Would God eternally judge when He hasn't given ability? A simple example of a father illustrates this notion. Would a loving earthly father spank a new born for not walking to him? I believe irresistible grace lessens God's love and grace from a gift to a requirement. God's love is so much greater when it is given, not forced. Prevenient grace is the most loving grace as demonstrated in the following verses: Exo. 33:19; Rom. 11:5-7 Tit. 2:11; Heb. 2:9; 4:16; 10:29; 12:15; Jam. 4:6; 1Pe. 1:13; 5:5, 10; Jud. 1:4; Acts 14:3; 20:24, 32; Rom. 5:2; 2Co. 4:15. What type of grace does God give?*—God's grace is enough for need *(salvation and sanctification). To whom does God give grace? God gives His grace to ALL who are in need).*

When appropriated by faith, Christ's death and burial provided <u>Redemption</u> or <u>Ransom</u> (bought back from sin, Satan, or death; **Mat. 20:28; 1Pe. 1:18; 1Ti. 2:6; Gal. 3:13**). His death provided <u>Propitiation</u> ("Satisfaction," because of the righteous payment, focusing on the God-ward side; **Rom. 5:10; 2Co. 5:18. 19; Eph. 2:16; Col. 1:20; Heb. 2:17**). His death provided <u>Reconciliation</u> (brought back into a right relationship, focusing on the man-ward side; **Rom. 5:10; 2Co. 5:18-19; Eph. 2:16; Col. 1:20; Heb. 2:17**). *God is propitiated, and man is reconciled and redeemed.*

Christ's Bodily Resurrection

The Bodily Resurrection of Jesus Christ is one of the greatest works that demonstrated His Deity (**Mat. 28:1-15; Mar. 16:1-14; Luk. 24:1-49; Joh. 20:1-23; Acts 1:1-11; 1Co. 15**). Jesus defeated our greatest enemy! His resurrection was witnessed by over 500 people that saw Him after His resurrection (**1Co. 15:4-8**). His Resurrection proves that Christ defeated sin, Satan, and the fear of death (**Heb. 2:14-15**). It proves that Christ has the power to bodily raise us from the dead as He promised (**1Th. 4:16**). Jn. 11:25-26 says, "Jesus said unto her, I am the Resurrection, and the Life: he that believeth in me, though he were dead, yet shall he live. And whosoever liveth and believeth in me shall never die. <u>Believest thou this</u>?" **Jn. 6:40** says, "And this is the will of him that sent me, that everyone which seeth the Son, and believeth on him, may have everlasting life: and I will raise him up at the last day."

Since the resurrection is true, there is no other religion or hope equal to it anywhere. For those who doubt its veracity, I challenge you to disprove it based on evidence. **Biblical authority** said so, before it happened, and after it happened. So, if you believe the Bible you will believe the resurrection. There are many credible **eye witnesses** (angels, women, apostles, miraculous signs, 500+, plus hostile witnesses. . .), where only two are needed in our courts. Josh McDowell (in his book, <u>Evidence that Demands a Verdict</u>) says,

"Those resources range from Josephus to a compilation of fifth century Jewish writings called the "Toledoth Jeshu." Dr. Paul Maier (1984 lecture at Dallas Theological Seminary) called this "positive evidence from a hostile source, the strongest kind of historical evidence. In essence, this means that if a source admits a fact, decidedly not in its favor, then that fact is genuine." Other evidence, including **circumstances** (empty tomb, no body, soldiers weren't executed as law required, Apostles gave lives). There are also **theological reasons** (sin produces death, and death can only hold sinners. God didn't sin, and God is life).

One of the strongest reasons for the Bodily Resurrection is that the best **theories against His resurrection** are woefully inadequate to explain this miraculous event. For example, in the Wrong Tomb theory everyone forgot and continued to go to the wrong tomb; thus, Jesus' dead body was really in a different tomb and He did NOT rise from the dead. *This would imply that all the family, women, Apostles, Jewish and Roman Authorities, Roman guards, etc. were wrong and could not produce His Body. Therefore, all people believed He did rise (with greater than 500 eye witnesses that saw Him after He rose)?* The mass hallucination theory suggests that Jesus did NOT rise, but people just thought they saw him around three days after He died because many said they saw Him. *This had none of the physiological or psychological principles for hallucination. Why couldn't anyone produce His body to prove to those who saw Him?* The stolen body theory suggests that the disciples of Jesus sneaked pass the soldiers, stole and hid His body somewhere else, and He really did NOT rise. Contrast this theory with the fact that *first, the disciples fled, denied, didn't believe, and acted cowardly. Why now would they be willing to fight Roman soldiers after He was dead, break the seal, roll a 4,000 lb. stone away, unwrap and carry Jesus' body past the guards, while no one else even saw them? Why would they do that and for what purpose? Why would they endure such persecution and eventually all not tell the truth, rather than die their recorded torturous deaths? If Jesus' body was stolen by the Jewish or Roman leaders, why wouldn't they say so, or show it when all were preaching and believing in the Resurrection of Jesus Christ?*

Finally, the <u>swoon</u> theory purports that Jesus wasn't really dead; He just pretended to be dead and simply walked out of the grave. *In reality, Christ, was so weak that He couldn't even carry His cross. He was beaten one stripe less than would kill, then nailed and crucified. Christ was verified dead by experts, and a spear pierced His side showing blood and water (proving death). He was then mummified. The swoon theory would suggest that three days later, without treatment, food, water, or infection, Jesus removed his own grave clothes, rolled a 4,000lb stone away by Himself (uphill), and fooled all His followers that He powerfully arose! The absurdity here is that the rulers didn't crucify, imprison, or kill Jesus when they found out. It also suggests that the guards didn't notice any of this, or weren't held accountable, and the Jews and Romans forgot to mention this oversight; and, of course, none of Jesus' enemies ever said this. It sure takes a lot of faith to refuse to believe in the historical resurrection of Jesus Christ.*

Another reason for the resurrection is the sheer **numbers who believe it** (thousands then, now about 75% of Americans, about 33% of the world...). One of the strongest reasons for the Resurrection is the changed lives of *those who believe in Jesus.* **Jesus has changed me** forever—*I see and feel His life in   Do you believe that Jesus is the Resurrection and the Life?* **Acts 17:32** says, "And when they heard of the resurrection of the dead, some mocked: and others said, 'We will hear thee again of this matter.'" *I believe it and bank my eternal life on it! How about you?*

Another miraculous work was the **Bodily Ascension and Exaltation** of Jesus (**Mar. 16:19-20; Luk. 24:50-53; Acts 1:9-11**). This returned Christ to His former glory and honor, ended His temporary self-limitation and placed Him at the right hand of the Majesty on High (**Eph. 1:20-23; Php. 2:9; Heb. 1:3**), and demonstrated how He will return to earth one day (**Acts 1:9-11**).

What is the **present work of Christ?** He is our: <u>Head</u> of the Church (**1Co. 12; Eph. 1:22-23; 5:23**), Great <u>High Priest</u> (**Heb. 4:14-16; 6:20; 8:1-5; 9:23-28**), <u>Intercessor</u> (**Rom. 8:34; Heb. 7:25**) *(prayer to keep us* *from sin)*, Advocate (**1Jo. 2:1 - 2**) *(Prayer to defend us when we sin)*, and the preparer of our heavenly home (**Joh. 14:2**).

His **future work** will be discussed in Eschatology, but five top works are listed below. (1) Rapture (**1Th. 4:13-18; 1Co. 15:52**)—**1Co. 15:52** says, "... in the twinkling of an eye ... " (any moment); **1Th. 4:17** says Christians will " ... meet the Lord in the air: and so shall we ever be with the Lord." (Christians won't have to leave Jesus again). (2) The Judgment Seat of Christ—**2Co. 5:10**; cf. **1Co. 3:11-15** *(a rewards ceremony for believers)*. (3) The 2nd Advent or 2nd Coming of Christ (**Mat. 24:16- 31; 1Th. 1:7-10; 2:8; Rev. 19:11-16**) *will occur seven years after the Rapture of the Church*. (4) The Millennial or Kingdom Reign (**Rev. 20:1-7**), *or the 1,000 year rule of Christ on earth)*. (5) The Great White Throne Judgment (**Rev. 20:9-15**) *is the judgment for unbelievers to be cast into Hell forever (see Eschatology to see how critical the work of Christ is in future events)*. *The last two verses of the Bible encourage all true believers in the **Rev. 22:20 - 21**—"... Surely I come quickly. Amen. Even So, come, Lord Jesus. The grace of our Lord Jesus Christ be with you all. Amen." What is your response to the fact that Jesus could come back at any moment? Are you ready? What is your prayer to Him today?*

God's eternal everywhere Spirit supernaturally draws, speaks, empowers, gifts, and desires to personally powerfully live in you.

Introduction

Pneumatology comes from the Greek stems *"Pneuma"*, meaning Spirit or breath, and *"logos"*, meaning a word about, the science of, or the study of; thus **Pneumatology is the study of the Holy Spirit.** A key verse is **Eph. 5:18**—"And be not drunk with wine, wherein is excess; but be filled with the Spirit."

Person—Deity

The Holy Spirit is called "God". **Acts 5:3**—" . . . why hath Satan filled thine heart to lie to the Holy Ghost . . . " **Acts 5:4**—" . . . thou hast not lied unto men, but unto God." "The Holy Spirit" is called "the Lord" (Adonai – a title for Yahweh). **Isa. 6:8-13**—"Also I heard the voice of the Lord, saying . . ." **Acts 28:25-27**—". . . Well spake the Holy Ghost by Isaiah the prophet unto our fathers . . ." (**Isa. 6:8** states "the Lord" said it, where **Acts 28:25** says "the Holy Spirit" said the Isaiah statement).

Titles and Names of God

The Holy Spirit is called the "Spirit **of God**" 26 times (**Rom. 8:9, 14**); "The Spirit **of the LORD**" is found 25 times (**Jdg. 3:10; 6:34; 11:29; 13:25; 14:6, 19**), "The Spirit **of the Lord**" is seen six times (**Isa. 61:1; Luk. 4:18; Acts 5:9; 8:39; 2Co. 3:17, 18**), "The Spirit **of the Lord God**" (**Isa. 61:1**), and "The Holy Spirit **of God**" (**Eph. 4:30**). **Isa. 61:1**—"The Spirit of the Lord GOD is upon me; because the LORD hath anointed me . . ." **1Jo. 5:7**—"For there are three that bear record in heaven, the Father, the Word, and the Holy Ghost: and these three are One."

Attributes of God

The Holy Spirit possesses all the attributes or characteristics of God. These are listed below: Spirituality—"God is Spirit" (**Joh. 4:24**). Omnipresence—without bodily boundaries; "Where shall I go from your Spirit" (**Psa. 139:7-13**). Omniscience—"The Spirit of wisdom and understanding"; "the Spirit of council"; "the Spirit of knowledge"; "the Spirit of . . . revelation" (**Exo. 31:3; Isa. 11:2; Eph. 1:17**). Omnipotence—"the Spirit of might" (**Isa. 11:2**). Life—"the Spirit of Life" (**Rom. 8:2; Rev. 11:11**). Truth—"the Spirit of Truth" (**Joh. 14:17; 15:26; 16:13; 1Jo. 4:6**). Grace—"the Spirit of Grace" (**Heb. 10:29; cf. Zec. 12:10**). Holiness—"the Spirit of Holiness" (**Rom. 1:4**); called "Holy" Spirit and there is none Holy, but God . . . "Holy Spirit"—six times (**Psa. 51:11; Isa. 63:10, 11; Luk. 11:13; Eph. 1:13; 4:30; 1Th. 4:8**). "Holy Ghost"—90 Times (**Luk. 1:35; 3:22 . . .**). Unity—"the unity of the Spirit" (**Eph. 4:3**); "one Spirit" (**Eph. 4:4**). *"The Spirit of Glory" (1Pe. 1:14) and "the Spirit of Adoption" (Rom. 8:15) show specific characteristics and actions of God.*

Refer to the Holy Spirit's works under the Trinity in Theology Proper section, as the Holy Spirit performs incommunicable works of God. The Holy Spirit can be sinned against (**Isa. 63:10; Acts 5:3, 5, 9; Mat. 12:32; Mar. 3:29; Eph. 4:30**). The Holy Spirit is a member of the Trinity (The Holy Spirit, the third Person of the Godhead). In the OT, plural names . . . e.g. "Elohim" (**Deu. 6:4**) and plural personal pronouns, such as "us," "our" (**Gen. 1:26 - 27; 11:7; Isa. 6:8**) were used of the Holy Spirit. In the NT, Christ's baptism (**Mat. 3:16-17**) had visible involvement by His Father and the Holy Spirit. Baptism for the Church to be ". . . baptizing them in the name of the Father, and of the Son, and of the Holy Ghost" clearly implies equality in the Godhead (**Mat. 28:19**). Paul's benediction purposely names the Holy Spirit, Christ, and God with the implication of equality—"The grace of the Lord Jesus Christ, and the love of God, and the communion of the Holy Ghost, be with you all. Amen" (**2Co. 13:14**). The Father is God (**Rom. 1:7; Joh. 1:18**), Christ is God (**Heb. 1:8; Joh. 1:1-18**), and the Holy Spirit is God (**Acts 5:3 - 4; 1Co. 2:9-10**).

Person

Many think of the Spirit as a force, not a **person** that has personality and personhood. The Holy Spirit is not just an impersonal or amoral influence, power, or force. He is a Person. This is contrary to Hinduism or other impersonal beliefs or philosophies that are man-centered. That is not the personal God, Who has thoughts, emotions, will, and acts personally. The Holy Spirit has personal characteristics and possesses the elements of personality in the following ways: (1) **Intellect (1Co. 2:10-11)** He ". . . searches, reveals, knows"; **Exo. 31:3**—He has knowledge, understanding, wisdom, (2) **Emotions (Eph. 4:30)** He can be "grieved", and (3) **Will (Acts 15:28)**— He decided; and **Acts 16:6**—He forbade).

The Spirit performs personal acts as He: (1) Descended from Heaven (**Luk. 3:22**), (2) Decided (**Acts 15:28**), (3) Forbade to preach at a certain place and time (**Acts 16:6**), (4) Appointed Overseers (**Acts 23:28**), (5) Sanctified (**Rom. 15:16**), (6) Spoke/Taught/Witnessed (**Mar. 13:11; Acts 13:2, 4; 20:23; 21:11; 28:25; 1Co. 2:13; Heb. 3:7; 9:8; 10:15** . . .), (7) Comforted (**Joh. 14:16; Acts 9:31**), (8) Communed (**2Co. 13:14**), and (9) Intercedes (**Rom. 8:26**). Additional works are listed below:

The Spirit has personal pronouns. It is true that the Greek word "pneuma" for spirit is neuter in gender as is a broadly used word also for the spirits of both men and women, for "wind" or "breath," but the Holy Spirit is referenced as masculine, e.g. "He" (**Joh. 15:26; 16:8, 13, 14, 15**), "Him" (**Joh. 16:7**), and "Himself" (**Joh. 16:13**).

Work

The Holy Spirit worked and continues to work in many ways. *His works, often misunderstood, are listed here by logical chronology.* In the OT, the Spirit was involved in the Divine counsel or Sovereign decrees of the Trinity to elect and predetermine all that was to come. Those decrees resulted in creation and preservation (**Gen. 1:2; Job 26:13; 33:4; Psa. 104:30**) by the Spirit. The Holy Spirit also provided temporary filling or miraculous empowerment in the OT with knowledge, understanding, and wisdom (**Exo. 31:3; 35:31**), revelation (**Num. 24:2f; 1Sa. 10:10**), prophecy (**Num. 11:25f; 1Sa. 10:11f**), and special acts (**Exo. 31:3f; Jdg. 14:19; 2Ki. 4**). *These were temporary acts of the Holy Spirit. King David in* **Psa. 51:11** *says, ". . . take not thy Holy Spirit from me." Here, David recognized the Holy Spirit's temporary filling, empowerment, and work in the OT.*

The Spirit's ministry spanned both the OT and NT periods with His progressive work in Scripture (see Bibliology for further explanation and permanency) including: (1) Revelation (**2Pe. 1:19-21**), (2) Inspiration (**2Ti. 3:16-17; 2Pe. 1:19-21**), (3) Transmission, (4) Canonization, (5) Translation, (6) Preservation (**Mat. 5:18; 24:35**), and (7) Illumination (**2Co. 4:2-6; 2Ti. 3:15; Pro. 1:7; 9:10; 1Co. 2:10-15; Psa. 19:8; Eph. 1:18**). *What a power and privilege we have to quote God's Word and to be guaranteed that the Holy Spirit will accomplish His purposes through the Word of God!*

The Spirit's Biblically recorded NT ministry started with the filling of John the Baptist, while even in His mother's womb. The baby John leaped in Mary's presence, and Elizabeth was filled with the Spirit and prophesied (**Luk. 1:15, 41**); *yet, here is another illustrative reference to life after conception and prior to birth.*

The Holy Spirit was involved in **Christ's**: conception (**Mat. 1:18-20; Luk. 1:34-35**), miracles (**Mat. 12:28**), and resurrection (**Rom. 8:11; 1Pe. 3:18**). He is involved in **drawing all believers and unbelievers to Christ** (**Joh. 12:32**) by miraculous work (usually through the saved) in the **Gospels, Rom. 15:19; Gal. 3:5**), reproving the world of sin, righteousness, and judgment (**Joh. 16:7-11**), and enlightening minds and understanding (**Eph. 1:17-20; Heb. 6:4**).

Spirit's Involvement with Unsaved

The Spirit is at work in the **unsaved**, even for those who reject the miraculous drawing by Holy Spirit. The unsaved resist the Holy Spirit (**Acts 6:10; 7:51; Rom. 13:2**). This is man attempting to counteract, defeat, or withstand the Holy Spirit, His purpose, and/or His works. *Can He be resisted? Acts 6:10 says in that they couldn't resist the Holy Spirit. Acts 7:51 says that the unsaved always resist the Holy Spirit as part of their continual rejection of God's revelation. Rom. 13:2 says that those resisting God's authorities will receive judgment.*

The Spirit restrains sin and sinners (**Gen. 6:3; 2Th. 2:7**). The Holy Spirit holds back, limits, restricts, impedes, places boundaries, detains, hinders, or keeps under restrains evil, or evil doers.

<u>"Blasphemy against the Holy Spirit"</u>—The Only Unpardonable Sin
People blaspheme the Holy Spirit (**Mat. 12:31-32; Mar. 3:29; Luk. 12:10**). What is the blasphemy against the Holy Spirit, and who can blaspheme? It is man speaking evil of, rejecting, or ascribing the Spirit's work elsewhere. *The Holy Spirit is invisible unless He inhabits or takes on the form of something like a "dove; " so can only see or respond to His work like the wind or breath, and ascribe it to something else, like Beelzebub or Satan or natural processes.*
<u>Definition</u> of blasphemy/ies/e/eth (34 times in Bible)—Hebrew - "nehawtsaw" (3 times in OT), "nawkab" (2 times in OT), and "nawats" (2 times in OT), "bawrak" (2 times in OT), and "gawdaf" (1 times in OT) means "scorn, blasphemy, puncture, perforate, libel, curse, pierce, strike through, abhor, despise, provoke, to curse God, hack (with words), revile, reproach" and Greek - "blasphemia" (16 times in NT) and "blasphemeo" (9 times in NT) means "vilification (especially against God), blasphemy, evil speaking, railing, to speak impiously, defame, revile".

<u>Key verses</u>—**Mat. 12:31-32** says, "Wherefore I say unto you, <u>All manner of sin and blasphemy shall be forgiven unto men</u>: but the blasphemy against <u>the Holy Ghost shall not be forgiven</u> unto men. And whosoever speaketh a word against the Son of man, it shall be forgiven him: but <u>whosoever speaketh against the Holy Ghost, it shall not be forgiven him</u>, neither in this world, neither in the world to come." **Mar. 3:28-29** says, "Verily I say unto you, <u>All sins shall be forgiven</u> unto the sons of men, and blasphemies wheresoever they shall blaspheme; but, he that shall <u>blaspheme against the Holy Ghost hath never forgiveness</u>, but is in danger of eternal damnation." **Luk. 12:10** says, "And whosoever shall speak a word against the Son of man, it shall be forgiven him; but unto him that <u>blasphemeth against the Holy Ghost it shall not be forgiven</u>."

What is "the Blasphemy against the Holy Spirit?" There are two key views: (1) <u>Some believe the blasphemy against the Holy Spirit to be a specific unpardonable sin</u>, or sins (murder, suicide, homosexuality, adultery, etc.). Some believe it can only be committed by the unsaved; others believe it can be committed by saved also and results in their losing their salvation (see Soteriology). *The Scriptures seem to clearly indicate that this view is invalid since Christ died for "all men" and all sin (**1Ti. 2:4, 6; 4:10; Tit. 2:11; Heb. 2:9; 1Jo. 2:2**). Since Christ died for all sin and paid for all sin, how is it that a certain sin wasn't paid for? It is clear from the next Scriptures that God has forgiven murder (**2Sa. 12:9, 13**), homosexuality, adultery, etc. (**1Co. 6:9-11**) and the passages say "all manner of sin shall be forgiven."*

(2) The second view of blasphemy against the Holy Spirit is attributed to speaking evil against the Holy Spirit's miraculous work. *Some like to parse words and say it is permitted to blaspheme or speak evil against God or Jesus, but not the Holy Spirit. Since they are all one God this parsing of words seems unfounded. It does make sense to say that when the Holy Spirit is doing a specific miraculous work in the hearts and minds of men, to reject to the point of verbally rejecting God's drawing is rejecting the Gospel. When a person continually or finally does so, this person will never be saved.* There are four views that are outgrowths of the second view stated above. There are listed briefly here:

a. Some well-known theologians (e.g. Dr. Dwight Pentecost; John MacArthur holds a modified view of this) believe that this blasphemy of the Holy Spirit was rejecting Christ's Kingdom offer to Israel and it cannot occur today. *Indeed, the Pharisees' sin was egregious in leading Israel to nationally reject and crucify Christ the King by ascribing Christ's miracles to Satan, and not to the Holy Spirit. Also there was an emphasis on the "Kingdom" in **Mat. 12:25-28**. This view, though widely held does not explain why people go to Hell today when the Scripture clearly indicate that "all manner of sin and blasphemy shall be forgiven unto men, except the blasphemy against the Holy Spirit." Are all going to heaven today? Clearly, the answer is unfortunately not all are going to heaven.*

b. Some good believers (often charismatics and Pentecostals) believe this sin to be generally rejecting Holy Spirit miracles as not from God. *This view is not widely held, but Christians who believe so urge others* to use great caution in disagreeing with their characterization of their believed miraculous experiences, frequently regarding the speaking in tongues. Several have expressed what was being evidenced in their church was the miraculous "gift of Tongues" given by the Holy Spirit as was clearly evidenced in the early NT Church. Those even using the Scriptural guidelines in 1Co. 14 to say that what they observed in their Church was not the Holy Spirit's working, since it was occurring contrary to Scripture, were greatly cautioned. This view maintains this could occur then and today, but it doesn't really explain the passage, forgiveness of sin, eternal security, or why speaking evil about the Holy Spirit is worse than speaking evil about God the Father or Son.

c. <u>Verbally attributing the Spirit's miracles done by Jesus to Satan</u> is the view that says Jesus was Satan incarnate, not God Incarnate. *This is well articulated by Kyle Butts in:* (*http://www.apologeticspress.org/articles/2272*). *Kyle says this could only happen while Jesus was physically performing miracles on earth and can't occur today. He also emphasizes that it must be verbally articulated; it is a "tongue sin". (See Confession under Soteriology for related discussion). He makes a strong point that "the Blasphemy against the Holy Spirit" isn't mentioned after the resurrection in Scripture, supporting his view that it couldn't happen today. "Blasphemy" is mentioned multiple times after the resurrection, but one could argue whether it was of the Holy Spirit or of God. This also is an argument from silence, so at best is weak. This view is strong, but doesn't really explain how all sin is paid for and forgiven today and many still go to Hell, or why a sin against the Holy Spirit is worse than sins against the Father and the Son.*

d. <u>Rejecting the Spirit's miraculous drawing to Christ</u> by speaking evil against or rejecting the Spirit's final proof that Jesus is God/Savior— even to extent of ascribing the Spirit's work to Satan or natural forces is <u>the final rejection of Christ</u> as Savior. *When the Spirit last miraculously draws one to Christ and gives one who is "dead in sins"* (**Eph. 2:1, 5; Col. 2:13**) *enough life and light to see and trust Christ, and they continue to "blaspheme", "speak evil against", reject the*

Spirit's miraculous enlightening work, they will never believe or be eternally saved. For those who claim the "blasphemy against the Spirit" can only be a "tongue sin," the context is much broader than that. Jesus in this passage is showing the Pharisee's escalating rejection in multiple ways. **Mat. 12:24** says, "And Jesus knew their thoughts. . ." **Mat. 12:34-35** says, ". . . how can ye, being evil, speak good things? For <u>out of the abundance of the heart the mouth speaketh</u>. A good man <u>out of the good treasure of the heart bringeth forth good things:</u> and an evil man <u>out of the evil treasure bringeth forth evil things</u>." This clearly shows this as a belief or heart matter, outwardly expressed and observed by others through the tongue; otherwise, we wouldn't know what God already knows and knew (see "confession" in Soteriology for additional discussion).

This view above fits the context of **Mat. 12** as the last proof the Holy Spirit gave to validate Jesus as God. The Pharisees had already rejected the witness and proof of the Law and Prophets, Father, and Son. The Holy Spirit was the final miraculous drawing and witness God could give. That is why rejecting or speaking evil of the "final work of the Holy Spirit" was the only sin that would not be forgiven; making its finality so much worse. All speaking evil of or rejecting God's outstretched miraculous arms to embrace them for eternity is horrible. However, only the last rejection against the Holy Spirit will bar an unsaved person from heaven. It is clear in the Gospels that from that point on, Christ spoke in parables concerning Himself and His kingdom. **Mat. 13** and the subsequent chapters consistently demonstrate Israelite leaders rejecting Christ. Some say it is a continuous rejection of Christ. Once the Spirit is blasphemed, they will never believe or be saved, and the Holy Spirit may never miraculously work in them again. This view seems to best fit the context of **Mat. 12** and **Mar. 3,** especially with an understanding of how God "draws all men" to Him (**Joh. 12:32**). It is consistent with the Gospel since there are no caveats. It is "Believe on the Lord Jesus Christ, and thou shalt be saved" (**Acts 16:31**). It is "But as many as received Him, to them gave He the power to become the sons of God" (**Joh. 1:12**). It is "He that believeth on Him is not condemned: but he that believeth not <u>is condemned already, because he hath not</u>

*believed in the name of the only begotten Son of God" (**Joh. 3:18**).
Though the word, "blasphemy" is not given in these verses, this view
of blasphemy is the most consistent and doesn't contradict the clear
gospel, or God's love and holiness. It is consistent with the eternal
security of the believer. It is consistent with the Holy Spirit's Work. It
is consistent with all other sin being forgiven, except rejecting or not
believing in Jesus. It is also interesting to note that those verses both
say that all sin will be forgiven "men," but not the angels, Devil, or
demons that fell. God does not offer fallen angels salvation. Angels
were in the very presence of God and pridefully rejected all that the
Spirit of God had shown them before falling. Man with lesser
spiritual understanding is Spirit enlightened to have that same
opportunity and choice.*

*In conclusion, what is "the blasphemy against the Holy Spirit"? I
believe it is the one and only unpardonable sin, or final rejection, or
unbelief. Is it a one-time event or can it occur on multiple occasions
continually? Does the Holy Spirit take a dead brain and "quicken,"
"enlighten," or "give it life" more than once in a person's life? I don't
know, but believe it is a one-time (last and final rejection). If a person
rejects more than once the Spirit's drawing, then it is both a continual
and final rejection. If the Spirit miraculously draws men only at one
point in their life, then it is both the first and final opportunity,
concurrently. The Spirit does work through God's Word every time to
accomplish His purposes. Men may blaspheme God continuously or
multiple times; but I am unsure if the Spirit enlightens multiple times
so that they could blaspheme the Spirit continuously. God's Word is
provided to unbelievers or rejecters in order to soften or harden
hearers, based on their response. Every time God's Word and the
plan of salvation is presented, and the Spirit speaks, it is serious. If a
person accepts the Spirit's drawing to Jesus, then there is confidence
that the Spirit has not been blasphemed.*

Spirit's Involvement with Saved

Where the unsaved rejected the Spirit's work with the disobedience
of unbelief, the saved receive the work of Holy Spirit with the
obedience of belief or faith. *The following all occur at the point of*

salvation (see Soteriology for great detail). The Spirit regenerates believers. Regeneration; "Born Again" (**Tit. 3:5; Joh. 3:3-7; 1Pe. 1:23**)—The Holy Spirit makes anew, renews, restores, or recreates; spiritual rebirth occurs at salvation only. The Spirit baptizes or Spirit Baptism (**Mat. 3:11; Mar. 1:8; Luk. 3:16; Act. 1:5; 4:16; 1Co. 12:12-13; Rom. 6:3-5**). There are five main Spirit baptism **views:**

1) **Holiness**—What: Cleansing of Spiritual corruption, up to spiritual perfection. How: Complete and full dedication to God. When: After salvation, frequently at water baptism or other dedication service. Recipients: Completely committed Christians. 2) **Reformed**—What: Spirit miraculous outpouring on Church fulfilling God's promise. How: God poured out Spirit on Church, evidenced through Miracles and Gifts. When: The Day of Pentecost (Acts 2) only. Recipients: Church only, not individual Christians. 3) **Charismatic/Pentecostal**—What: Spirit's miraculous empowering, calling, or gifting (believe "fruit" or "tongues" is a sign of baptism). How: At or after salvation the Spirit pours out power or gifting. When: At spiritual maturity, upon a special anointing by a Christian leader or church, as the Spirit is ready, normally believed separate from salvation; some believe can occur multiple times. Recipients: Saved and yielded Christians. 4) **Catholic/Church of Christ**—What: Spirit placing one into Christ's body (Church), regenerating, and enlightening for Christian life. How: Belief in Jesus and water baptism. When: When water baptized. Recipients: Catholics, Church of Christ, and others that believe in baptismal regeneration (see Soteriology) or water baptism as a Sacrament, not just as an Ordinance (see Ecclesiology). 5) **Correct**—What: Spirit placing one into Christ's Body eternally. How: Belief in Jesus. When: one - time at salvation. Recipients: Christians only. Further Defined: A singular act (begun at Pentecost) only at the point of salvation, where the Holy Spirit places a believer into the body of Christ by spiritually identifying, uniting, and burying them in Christ's death and raising them to walk in newness of life. *"For by one Spirit are we all baptized into one body"* (**1Co. 12:13**b) *shows that all Christians are Spirit baptized. Nowhere are believers commanded to pray for or be Spirit baptized, indicating that Spirit baptism already happened to all believers. Nowhere does it say Spirit*

baptism ever happened more than once in a believer's life. A one-time Spirit baptism demonstrates and shows what and how the Spirit united us with Christ and other believers at salvation. Spirit baptism literally accomplishes what water baptism symbolizes, represents, and testifies that Spirit baptism occurred. I believe water baptism by immersion best pictures what spiritually took place at salvation. We were completely buried with Christ's death and completely raised by His resurrection power over sin and death. Some see water baptism also a commitment to follow Jesus as Lord, not just a testimony of Spirit baptism. (See Soteriology for more detail).

The Spirit indwells believers. Indwelling (**Joh. 14:16-17**; **Rom. 8:9-11**; **1Co. 3:16**; **6:19-20**; **2Ti. 1:14**)—The Holy Spirit takes up permanent residence, dwells in, and remains in a believer's life at the point of salvation. Sealing (**2Co. 1:22**; **Eph. 1:13**; **4:30**)—The Holy Spirit's one-time (at the point of salvation) marking, securing, confirming, attesting, ratifying, confirming, guaranteeing, authenticating, and assuring a believer of their eternal relationship with God through Jesus Christ. Justification (**1Co. 6:11**)—The Holy Spirit (at the point of salvation) placing a believer in Christ to legally declare them 100% righteous; not only "Just-If-I'd never sinned", but "Just-If-I'd always performed everything perfectly"; not just sinless, but perfect, the righteousness of Christ by the Holy Spirit.

Spiritual Gifts

The Spirit is a gracious giver of Spiritual Gifts (**Rom. 12**: **1Co. 12**; **Eph. 4**; **1Pe. 4**). Some selected Scriptures (underlining mine for emphasis). **1Co. 12:1, 4, 7, 11, 13, 31**—1. "Now concerning spiritual gifts, brethren, I would not have you ignorant." 4. "Now there are diversities of gifts, but the same Spirit." 7. "But the manifestation of the Spirit is given to every man to profit withal." 11. "But all these worketh that one and the selfsame Spirit, dividing to every man severally as He will." 13. "For by one Spirit are we all baptized into one body, whether we be Jews or Gentiles, whether we be bond or free; and have been all made to drink into one Spirit." 31. "But covet earnestly the best gifts: and yet shew I unto you a more excellent way." **1Co. 13:8**—Spiritual Gifts "shall cease," but "love never faileth."

Some divide the gifts as either ministry or miraculous or sign gifts. I believe them all to be miraculous. All views believe "the Spiritual Gifts" were active. All believe they will "cease," "vanish away," and "be done away" when they have accomplished their purpose (**1Co. 13:8-10**). It is just a matter of when they will or did cease. God doesn't want us ignorant regarding our place in His body, the Church, and our role by how He has gifted us with Spiritual Gifts. We have different Gifts, but one Spirit. Gifts are the way the Spirit manifests Himself to Christians and the world. Spiritual Gifts are given to profit ALL. The Spirit works in all the exercising of the Spiritual Gifts. Christians have been gifted the way the Spirit wants us to work. All those with Spiritual Gifts have been Spirit baptized first into Christ's one body (they were saved and identified spiritually with His death, burial, and resurrection). There are no racial, spiritual, or social dividers in the one Spirit that allowed us to be unified in the Body of Christ. Desire the best Spiritual Gifts and do all in accordance with the two top commands, "love." Spiritual Gifts are love Gifts to be exercised in love in and through Christ's Body, the Church (**1Co. 13**).

Spiritual Gifts listed in alphabetical order including some context. Apostleship (**1Co. 12:28-29; Eph. 4:11**), Discernment (**1Co. 12:10**), Evangelism (**Eph. 4:11**), Exhortation / Encouragement (**Rom. 12:8**) wait on exhortation (**Rom. 12:8**), Faith (**1Co. 12:9; 13:2**), Giving (**Rom. 12:8; 1Co. 13:2**) give "with simplicity" (**Rom. 12:8**), Government / Ruling (**Rom. 12:8; 1Co. 12:28**) Rule "with diligence" (**Rom. 12:8**), Healings (**1Co. 12:9, 28, 30**), Hospitality[2] (**1Pe. 4:9**), Interpretation (of Tongues) (**1Co. 12:10, 30**), Knowledge (**1Co. 12:8; 13:2**), Mercy (**Rom. 12:8**) show mercy "with cheerfulness" (**Rom. 12:8**), Ministry / Helps / Administration / Service (**Rom. 12:7; 1Co. 12:28; 1Pe. 4:11**) "let us wait on our ministering" (**Rom. 12:7**); minister "as of the ability which God giveth," Miracles (**1Co. 12:10, 28-29**), Prophecy / Speaking[3] (**Rom. 12:6; 1Co. 12:10, 28-29; 13:2; Eph. 4:11**) "prophesy according to proportion of faith" (**Rom. 12:6**); speak "as of the oracles of God" (**1Pe. 4:11**), Pastoring / Teaching[4]

(**Rom. 12:7; 1Co. 12:28-29; Eph. 4:11; 1Pe 4:11**) wait on teaching (**Rom. 12:7**), Tongues (**1Co. 12:10, 28, 30; 13:1; 14**) with unsaved, pray he may interpret, and Wisdom (**1Co. 12:8; 13:2**).

[1]: All passages and use of the Spiritual Gifts are found within the context of "love."

*[2]: Hospitality is listed within the Gifts' passages (**Rom. 12:13; 1Pe. 4:9**), but not clearly specified whether it was a Gift or just a way of exercising the Gifts.*

[3]: Speaking is listed among Gifts and "oracles of God" make it sound as if it was referring to Prophecy (rather than other speaking Gifts like Pastoring / Teaching, Tongues...).

*[4]: Pastoring / Teaching are sometimes considered separate gifts since it is specified three times as Teaching and only one time (**1Pe. 4:11**) as Pastoring and Teaching (one Greek word, not two). It is also frequently referred to as Pastor / Teacher in the literature, which focuses more on the office or position, rather than the actual evidencing of the Gift.*

Sanctification

Sanctification means to purify, make holy, or set apart (**Rom. 15:16; 2Th. 2:13; 1Pe. 1:2**). There are four main types or stages of sanctification. Pre-Salvific (part of the drawing process or setting apart), Positional (at salvation), Progressive (as we yield to the Spirit and confess sin—cf. **Rom. 6-8; 1Jo. 1:9**), and Permanent (when ultimately glorified in heaven).

Filling of the Spirit

Spirit filling (**Acts 2:4; Eph. 5:18; Luk. 1:15, 41, 67**) has both positive and negative actions and responses by believers. Positively, a believer can walk, live, or be led by the Spirit (**Gal. 5:16, 18, 25; Rom. 8:14**) and evidence fruit (**Gal. 5:22-23**). These positive results have strong parallels, or the same results as being filled with Scripture (**Eph. 5:19; Col. 3:16**); "the Spirit of Truth" (**Jn. 14:17; 15:26; 16:13**) and "the Word of Truth" (**Jn. 17:17-19; 2Co. 6:7; Ep. 1:13; 2Ti. 2:15; James 1:18**). Negatively, a believer can grieve or resist the Spirit (**Eph. 4:30**), can quench (**1Th. 5:19**), or also have or produce negative fruit (**Gal. 5:17 - 21**).

The Spirit's Direct Work

The Spirit <u>witnesses</u> or <u>testifies</u> of Jesus (**Joh. 15:26; Acts 5:32; 20:23; Rom. 8:16; Heb. 10:15; 1Pe. 1:12**). He <u>anoints</u> (**2Co. 1:21; 1Jo. 2:20, 27**), <u>teaches</u> (**Luk. 12:12; Joh. 14:26; 1Co. 2:10-14**), <u>guides</u>, <u>leads</u>, <u>directs</u>, <u>calls</u>, <u>sends</u> (**Joh. 16:13; Acts 8:29; 13:2,4; 16:6; Rom. 8:14**), <u>comforts</u> (**Joh. 14:16-26; 15:26; 16:7; Acts 9:31**), and <u>intercedes</u> (**Rom. 8:26-27**).

Spirit's End Times Work

The Bible prophesies of the Spirit's <u>miraculous outpouring</u> reviving in the <u>Tribulation</u>, where His OT ministry resumes (cf. **Acts 2:17-21; Zec. 12:10, etc.**) and in the <u>Millennium</u> to enable Israel to <u>live righteously</u> (**Eze. 36:27**) and for all to experience Christ's <u>righteous rule</u> with knowledge, understanding, wisdom, counsel, and might (**Isa. 11:2**f). *The Spirit's end time's work may be a combination of the Spirit's OT, NT, and Heavenly ministry.*

Special creation, not evolved animal; man can only be fully satisfied by trusting intimacy with God; who are we, from where did we come, what is our purpose, and where are we going?

Introduction

Anthropology comes from the Greek stems *"Anthropos"*, meaning man, and *"logos"*, meaning a word about, the science of, or the study of; thus **Anthropology is the study of Man or Mankind**. Some key verses are **Gen. 1:26-27** which says, "And God said, Let us make man in our image, after our likeness: and let them have dominion over the fish of the sea, and over the fowl of the air, and over the cattle, and over all the earth, and over every creeping thing that creepeth upon the earth. So God created man in his *own* image, in the image of God created he him; male and female created he them."

Origin of Man

Where did we come from? The two most popular theories are Evolution and Creation. Interestingly enough, creationism was the only theory taught in American schools as our country was founded on a belief in God (as the Declaration of Independence reminds that we get our rights from "Nature's God . . . that all Men are created equal, that they are endowed by their Creator . . ."). Years after the famous Scopes Trial (1925) in the 1960's, some schools began teaching evolution. In 1987, many states taught, and some states had laws requiring the teaching of Creation, but the Supreme Court ruled this as establishing a religion by the state. From that point on, only private and home schools were legally permitted to teach creation, even if creation was only taught alongside evolution. Most Americans still claim to believe in Creation and many now attempt to believe in both creation and evolution. Let's briefly examine both theories.

Theory of Evolution

Evolution: Billions of years ago, lifeless matter was acted upon by natural forces, which by chance gave rise to all living things, developing up to man. Man in his entirety is a complete result of chance and evolution. Someone described it as, "From goo to you, by way of zoo." There are those who believe in Atheistic or Theistic evolution.

Atheistic Evolution Theory

Atheistic Evolution says that there is no God and only natural processes were involved. The two most popular theories are Steady State and the famous Big-Bang theory. **Steady State**: The universe eternally existed, but then changed and everything, including man, evolved into being. **Big-Bang**: A single magnanimous mass of eternally existing matter somehow exploded propelling fragments into space which after billions of years resulted in galaxies, stars, planets, and everything else, including life and man. Tragically, Charles Darwin began as a conservative, literally believing the Bible and God, went to seminary, then married his cousin Emma Wedgwood, had several frail children die, and struggled with how God would allow evil in the world. These feelings of desperation led to his liberal and famous theory of evolution in 1859 (On the Origin of Species). His big theories included natural selection in the breeding process (survival of the fittest) and transmutation of the species (or species change). Both Steady State and Big-Bang evolutionary theories use similar arguments to support their theories.

Evolutionary Arguments and Answers

Let's examine some of the top arguments of evolution. **Comparative Anatomy and Embryonic Capitulation**: If things didn't evolve, then why are living creatures so similar in their early development? One Creator made all things to live in a similar environment; hence, there would be similarities and commonalties in appearance and early development.

Human DNA versus Chimpanzee DNA: The Human Genome Project (www.genome.gov) was successfully completed in 2003. You've probably heard that 98% of human DNA is similar to a chimp (now it is known to be about 95%). What you haven't heard is that most

DNA is similar to all life and creation or the difference in Chromosomes (man 46, chimps 48). Also conveniently not mentioned are the different DNA types and functions, and the vast quantities we are talking about. There are about 3 billion base pairs in the human genome, so even 5% is a difference of about 150 million. If you were to line up all the DNA found in every cell of a human body it would stretch about 9.3 billion miles or 372,000 times around the earth. Obviously, life on earth requires somewhat similar DNA sequences. Even more silent is the fact that scientists now generally conclude that there is a recent single origin for man, which the Bible calls Adam. If you found a spilled bowl of alphabet soup and saw "Hey Dad" lined up perfectly on the floor, would you believe those six letters were sequenced that way by accident or that someone intelligently and intentionally positioned them that way? DNA sequences for only one person would be similar to finding thousands of bowls spilled and hundreds of volumes of encyclopedias showing up, without error. Truly, DNA is an incredibly strong argument for Intelligent Design (creation), and not accidental incredible complexity (see Theology Proper, Teleological section).

Vestigial Organs: Why are there so many unneeded organs in man? Science once maintained many useless organs existed because we could remove them without death, but modern science is discovering many important functions in organs formerly thought worthless (tonsils, appendix, etc.). **Natural Selection** or **Survival of the Fittest**: Why do the strongest seem to breed more if this isn't a completely natural part of evolution? An intelligent God designed His creation in order that the strongest and most helpful traits in a species and an environment would be passed on to the next generation.

Mutations: Mutations prove a possible mechanism for things to get better. True mutations occur and historically disappear quite suddenly. Mutations are rarely beneficial and are generally weaker. Even if it isn't a negative mutation, mutated organisms are normally sterile (cannot reproduce or get passed on). Even if a mutated organism could reproduce, it does not transmit the mutation. Scientists attempting to prove evolution by the possibility of mutational enhancement usually just work with recessive genes and usually artificially produce and keep them alive. **Transmutations:** Transmutations must exist for evolution to have taken place (species must change across species). There have been changes within species adapting to their environments, but in all of the recorded world history, there has never ever been a change from one species to another.

Paleontology: Isn't the fossil record the strongest evidence of evolution over time? No, actually it is the strongest evidence against evolution. If evolution were true, there should be thousands of simple fossils in many layers of stratification, then slowly more and more complex fossils arising after lots of deposits of sediment. The fossil records show a sudden appearance of life, contrary to the evolutionary model. Simple and complex fossils appear together, when the evolutionary model requires the simple fossils to appear millions of years prior to the complex fossils. There are no transitional fossils, which is essential to the theory of evolutionary model requiring big jumps from species to species that have never been observed or proven. What about *uniformitarianism* (the rate of sediment deposit is the same)? Does that prove more time? Evolution is not the only theory that explains fossil formation and age. Are the ages of rocks determined independently of the evolutionary premise? For example, an evolutionist may assume a fossil is 100,000,000 years old, and when another one is found in the same strata or has the same carbon dating they assume it must be the same age. All dating methods thus far have been proven ineffective (e.g. even claiming that a living turtle was over 14,000 years old with carbon dating). God quite obviously created a mature universe (fruit trees, animals, man, rocks...not seeds and babies). Age determination is performed either by witnesses or comparison with other similar things. Even natural events change appearance and create the pressure exerted upon rocks from earthquakes, volcanoes, lightning, floods, etc. that provide even more than the appearance of age. A common assumption that a hundred foot thick coral reef required millions of years to exist (evolutionists assume current rates of growth and reproduction and have always existed or that 90 feet were not created by God to begin with to support life). An assumption that other minerals or maybe large diamonds require many years of pressure and *aging* on coal, as compared to God creating it are predicated upon a belief in evolutionary theory.

Missing Link(s): Hasn't man discovered dozens of "missing links" proving transition from one species to another as evolutionary theory maintains? Although dozens have been claimed with entire drawings, dummies, and frameworks of hairy, ape-boned, progressively taller, and more erect and less hairy men have been reported and published, they have all been scientifically shown as hoaxes. One of the most famous, the "Piltdown Man" from Piltdown, East Sussex England, was touted and displayed worldwide for 41 years until proven to have been an intentional combination from parts of an orangutan and human skull. It is also interesting to note that with sometimes 50 or 60 biology book revisions, I haven't seen any retractions concerning this evidence. A logical conclusion for evolutionary theory requires the majority of fossils to be "transitional" fossils, or missing links, but that is not the case. Evolution has many gaps (missing links) to find if it is to be considered intelligible. Not only does evolution have missing links; it has a missing chain.

Evolution is just a theory and does not even scientifically meet the requirements of a theory, or the scientific method (observation, measurement, experiment, and form, test, and modify hypotheses). Evolution attempts to come up with an alternative to believing in God. Man doesn't want to feel responsible to someone besides himself. Evolution has no explanation of the origin of life. Evolution cannot even explain the method by which it works; it has no visible evidence of its occurrence today, or ever. This is why evolutionists must claim that it takes billions of years for this process to have been even statistically possible.

Evolution contradicts Universal Laws, which they affirm. The Law of Biogenesis or Abiogenesis: Life only comes from life; life cannot come from non-life (death). The 2nd Law of Thermodynamics or Law of Entropy: Everything has a tendency to disorder or decay, not getting better, but worse. God calls it the Law of Sin and Death. Evolution cannot explain the immaterial part of man (reason, mind, morals, values, spirit, soul, conscience, emotions).

What are the chances of one man evolving from gas or even a simple celled creature? We'll have to assume simple celled creatures and the universe already existed for them to live. Now, suppose that this actually happened after trillions of years (since there has been no record of even one species change along the way). Does it seem even remotely possible that a woman would evolve simultaneously and 'breed' before that man would have died out, never to be seen again?

Atheistic Evolution has NO Scriptural basis (**Gen. 1-2**). **Gen. 1:1** says, "In the beginning God created the heaven and the earth." **Joh. 1:3** says, "All things were made by him; and without him was not anything made that was made." **Col. 1:16** says, "For by him were all things created, that are in heaven, and that are in earth, visible and invisible, whether *they be* thrones, or dominions, or principalities, or powers: all things were created by him, and for him." **Heb. 11:3** says, "Through faith we understand that the worlds were framed by the word of God, so that things which are seen were not made of things which do appear."

Theistic Evolutionary Theory

Theistic Evolution: God initially used evolution by plan and design (supernatural and natural processes). This usually emanates from a Deistic or accommodation philosophy. Theistic evolution includes: (1) **Progressive Creationism**: This allows for more intervention and control by God; and (2) **Threshold Evolution**: God created the "kinds." There are gaps between the "kinds," and things evolved out of the "kinds." This view believes the "scientific data" supports this theory. This seems an attempt (primarily by Christians) to reconcile the Bible with science as they have been taught both as absolute. They are usually unaware of the scientific support for Creationism or have bought into some of the alleged evolutionary claims. This seems to try to compromise between Atheistic Evolution and Theistic Creationism, which will satisfy neither as the underlying philosophical beliefs are diametrically opposed. Theistic evolutionists <u>believe the universe is billions of years old</u>. A review of the history for any culture eventually proves that the majority buys many falsities when repeated enough, and unfortunately, the majority are going to Hell. They believe evolution takes place today. It clearly does not take place in its religious or philosophical meaning as is being claimed. Change clearly occurs, as a wise God certainly made His creation very adaptable for survival, but creatures do not change entire entities or species. God doesn't need the evolutionary process. This also seems to be **incompatible with the doctrines of the Fall and Redemption** (see Hamartiology and Soteriology).

<u>Theistic Evolution has NO Scriptural basis</u>. There is no Scriptural support, in fact, the opposite is strongly stated. **Gen. 2:2** says, "And on the seventh day God ended His work which He had made; and He rested on the seventh day from all His work which He had made." **Gen. 2:7** says, "And the LORD God formed man *of* the dust of the ground, and breathed into his nostrils the breath of life; and man became a living soul." **Gen. 2:23** says, "And Adam said, This *is* now bone of my bones, and flesh of my flesh: she shall be called Woman, because she was taken out of Man." **1Co. 15:39** says, "All flesh *is* not the same flesh: but *there is* one *kind of* flesh of men, another flesh of beasts, another of fishes, *and* another of birds." **Psa. 33:9** says, "For He spoke, and it was done, He commanded, and it stood fast."

Creationism

Creation: At the beginning of time, the eternally existing God created all that exists according to His plan and purpose! Man in his entirety is a complete result of God's divine image and workmanship. A great resource that provides numerous current scientific research and extensive evidence demonstrating creation is the Institute for Creation Research (http://www.icr.org). ICR has thousands of Christian scientists and lists their principles of scientific creationism and their amazing findings that aren't even mentioned in most American tax funded schools today (*yet another sad reason why*

America continues to lag behind less developed nations in math and science each year; see http://www.bloomberg.com/news/2010-12-07/teens-in-u-s-rank-25th-on-math-test-trail-in-science-reading.html, where the U.S. ranked 25th out of 34 countries).

<u>Old Earth Creationists</u>
Some godly creationists maintain an old earth or universe consistent with popular geological views, without evolution. The two most popular views are Day Age and Gap Theories. <u>Day Age</u> holds the six days of creation were not literal 24-hour days, but unknown ages or periods. They cite **Psa. 90:4** and **2Pe. 3:8**, which shows God's eternality and patience in judgment with words like: "one day is with the Lord as a thousand years, and a thousand years as one day." I don't hold this as those two verses are a clear literal simile using "as" in comparison and the Genesis creation account does not do that. Also, never does Scripture use the Hebrew "*Yom*" (day) proceeded by a number where it is not a literal 24-hour day, and it isn't consistent with "the" Sabbath Day (only a day), God certainly still isn't resting on "the" seventh day (for thousands, millions, or billions of years), and God didn't need time for a supernatural creation.

The <u>Gap Theory</u>, Gap Creation, or Ruin Reconstruction view holds that between **Genesis 1:1** and **1:2** there was an unknown gap of time (between a believed original creation and its ruin or destruction) resulting in reconstruction. Most frequently cite Satan's Fall in sin and to earth as rationale for earth's ruin. I don't hold this view as God begins the Bible in **Gen. 1:1** with "In the beginning, God created the heavens and the earth" as an introduction or thesis statement that He then describes the six days of creation in chapters one and two. Also **Gen. 1:2** says, "And the earth was without form and void…" The Hebrew "*waw*" (and) is a continuation of the thought as exists on all the verses in the creation account. Also Gap adherents want to change the word (KJV) "was" to "became" to support their attempt to accommodate some geologist timelines of an old earth. Also God says He created the earth in six days, "For in six days the LORD made heaven and earth, the sea, and all that in them is, and rested the seventh day" (**Exo. 20:11; 31:17**) and the Bible and Jesus never say there were two creations or a creation and restoration. Most proponents also believe dinosaurs . . . died out prior to the "restoration". The Bible says that sin and death came about from Adam: "by one man sin entered into the world and death by sin" (**Gen. 5:12**). Also the Bibles does not say this, God didn't need it, and a literal straight forward reading of the creation account makes sense on its own without any other accommodation attempt.

How Old is the Universe

Time of Creation: Archbishop Usher estimated the earth to be about 4004 B.C. from the genealogies listed in the Bible. The Bible sometimes uses ancestral lineages ("descendent of," not necessarily "son of" or "daughter of"). This is demonstrated in several known places in Scripture where it is summarizing blood lines or direct royal relationships. There are many theories based upon a "young earth" position. Many maintain creation was anywhere from 5,000 to 10,000 years ago. A young earth maintains the "appearance of age" (created Latin: *ex nihilo* "out of nothing," *which is what Creation is*) and was necessary in creation to provide man an environment and world with what was needed for sustainment. Regardless of the actual age of the universe, or the appearance of age it was given, the miracle of God's creation is apparent. I have worked many years at NASA and frequently one of the most difficult intellectual questions of both Christians and atheists pertains to the age of the universe. If you research the Hubble Space Telescope (http://hubblesite.org), you will see mentioned that it takes billions of years for light to travel so that some of what we observe of our gigantic universe can even get a glimpse of distant galaxies. Many conclude that these stars and galaxies died out billions of years before the earth was even formed. This is based on the assumption of the time it takes light to travel that far (*the speed of light is a known constant of 186,282 miles per second when traveling in the fairly consistent vacuum of space*). NASA is trying to develop the James Webb Space Telescope (JWST) to be able to use infrared to penetrate clouds, cosmic dust, etc., to peer farther out and into what is considered our universe's past (*that is believed not to even exist anymore*). This troubled me (as a young earth proponent) until I read the Biblical creation account recently.

It demonstrates that God solved this problem again with the "appearance of age" and the miracle of creation. **Genesis 1:3-5** says that God (again out of nothing) created the appropriate "light" on Day 1 of creation and not until Day 4 did He create the sun, moon, stars, etc. (**Gen. 1:14-19**). This means the light required for earth observers to see them was specially created; so, additional extra time was unneeded, including the 8 minutes and 19 seconds it takes light to reach earth from our sun. It is an amazing miracle that God created light, time, and space for us and the rest of His creation!

Science versus Faith

For those who say that Evolution is scientific and Creation is religious. Both are belief systems. The U.S. Supreme Court removed the state sponsorship of Creation teaching, when Evolution was permitted. Now Evolution is the state sponsored belief system that now indoctrinates our children in our tax funded public schools, forbidding Creation to also be taught. Which is more intellectually honest and fair, to teach both as theories and let children and families make up their own mind or to force one upon all without permitting the other? Which really is establishing a belief system? Also, which really takes more faith or is more scientific? Evolution— Somehow, something, somewhere, eternally existed, denies universal laws (never observed to be broken), keeps getting better until man evolves, all the evidence disappears, and it is not observed today; and, we have life, love, but no real purpose... Or, an eternal personal God created man in His own image with eternal purpose! What do you believe and choose?

Original State of Man

What is our purpose? The Bible says that God created man in His "image" and "likeness" (**Gen. 1:26-27; 2:7; 5:1-3**). He created us innocent and "very good" (**Gen. 1:31**) and Adam and Eve didn't even know they were naked (**Gen. 2:25; 3:7**). What is God's image and likeness? The Bible doesn't say explicitly. It does reveal a lot about God's personality, His attributes, His love, His holiness, His mind, His passions, His actions, His dominion, His desire to have a relationship with man, His creation of marriage and family, His creativity and plans. We see ourselves communicating with languages, desiring deeply satisfying relationships, seeking true love, wanting power, glory, and fame, expressing our creativity, desiring a family, using our minds, feeling deeply, seeking our purpose. This is further proof that we have come from God and not from unintelligent, unemotional, non-purposeful eternal gases. Furthermore, where would these gases have come from? God says that our purpose is <u>to love and glorify our Creator God first, and then man</u> (**Mat. 22:36-40; 7:12; Joh. 13:34-35; 1Co. 10:31; Col. 3:17, 23; Eph. 1:12**).

Marriage and Family

God instituted marriage of one man and one woman for life on earth, but not heaven (**Gen. 1:26-27**; cf. **Mat. 22:30**). The family was created as the societal cornerstone for the purpose of populating God's earth and having dominion over it (**Gen. 1:22, 28; 8:17; 9:1, 7**). Let it be said here that heterosexual, homosexual, or any other sex outside of marriage is sin (**1Co. 6:18; 7:2; 10:8; Gal. 5:19; Ex. 20:14; Lev. 18:22; 20:10, 13; Rom. 1:24-32**, etc.). Besides God's commands and ideal design, marriage saves great emotional pain, physical diseases (many auto-immune and some treatable and untreatable venereal diseases), and the entire world's human population would die out in one generation if all were homosexual. God created Adam and Eve, not Adam and Steve. God created woman, the perfect and suitable complement (not competition) for man, to be a companion and help in populating and being a steward of God's beautiful creation (**Gen. 2:18, 21-23**), even naming everything (**Gen. 2:19-20**). God Himself instituted marriage between one man (husband) and one woman (wife) and sanctified and made honorable nakedness and sex ("one flesh") only in that context without guilt or shame (**Gen. 2:24; Heb. 13:5**). God designed sex to be beautiful, fulfilling, and a special intimacy builder between the husband and wife. This family picture helps us understand love, authority, responsibility, and the unity and care of God. Marriage of the husband and wife is the perfect portrayal of Christ and the Church, His bride (**Eph. 5:23-33**), who in heaven will become Christ's wife (**Rev. 21:9**).

What is our <u>unique make-up and composition</u>? Are we just the average of our physical 20 main elements that currently total about $4.50 (oxygen, carbon, hydrogen, nitrogen, calcium, phosphorous, potassium, sulfur, sodium, chlorine, magnesium, iron, iodine, and trace minerals of fluorine, silicon, manganese, zinc, copper, aluminum, and arsenic)? Many physicians, psychologists, and theologians jointly discuss man as either as a dichotomy or trichotomy). <u>Dichotomy</u>: Man consists of two non-overlapping parts (material or body and immaterial or spirit/soul). <u>Trichotomy</u>: Man consists of three non-overlapping parts (material or body and separates immaterial into soul and spirit). Many great Christians hold each view. *I hold the trichotomy view due to two verses that call them out separately.* **1Th. 5:23**—". . . I pray God your <u>whole spirit</u> and <u>soul</u> and <u>body</u> be preserved blameless unto the coming of our Lord Jesus Christ." **Heb. 4:12**—"For the word of God is quick, and powerful, and sharper than any two-edged sword, piercing even to the <u>dividing asunder</u> of <u>soul</u> and <u>spirit</u>, and of the <u>joints and marrow</u>, and is a discerner of the thoughts and intents of the heart."

When we speak of the <u>material aspects</u> of man, the NT uses the Greek: *soma* - "body" and sometimes *sarx* - "flesh"* (although normally referring to the immaterial old nature), which just refers to what we all see of our skin, flesh, organs, systems, and bones; the "<u>outward man</u>." This body has senses (seeing, hearing, smelling, tasting, touching, and various others related to balance, temperature, movement, pain, time). The Bible says our physical body perishes or dies (**2Co. 4:16; Heb. 9:27**) and will be resurrected (**1Co. 15:40f**). *See eschatology for multiple and more detailed resurrections of saved and unsaved.*

When we discuss the <u>immaterial aspects</u> or capacities of man or the "inward man," it is more intensely debated as was demonstrated by the two main views above. What are the possible elements of the immaterial parts of man? 1) <u>Soul</u> (Greek: *psuche*)—soul, breath, spirit, heart, life, mind, emotions, feelings, personality; 2) <u>Spirit</u> (Greek: *pnuema*)—spirit, breath, life, mind, thinking, will; 3) *<u>Flesh</u> (Greek: *sarx*)—can be external flesh, but also human nature, <u>inward</u>

92

nature, "old nature," or "old man" that describes our natural fleshly needs turned into lustful cravings (**Rom. 6:6; 7:24; 8**); and 4) New nature or "new man" that describes a Christian's new life and desires as a believer (**Eph. 4:24; Col. 3:10; 2Co. 5:17**). It is interesting that the soul, spirit, flesh, old nature, new nature, with the intellect (mind), emotions (feelings/sensibility), will (choice/volition), and conscience (guilt) seem to individually combine to make each person unique and far above the animals. Man is the creature that God designed like Him, to intimately relate and personally live with Him for all eternity (see Soteriology).

There are three main views or theories of the origin of our soul/spirit or how we get our immaterial, the real you. (1) Pre-existence (Hinduism, Theosophy, heathen religions and philosophies; reincarnation—more of a recycling view of the soul); (2) Traducianism (it is passed on by parents; sometimes questioned regarding Jesus Christ and the passing of the sin nature—*see Hamartiology*); and (3) Creationism (God miraculously creates a new one at birth). Clearly the Bible does not teach the pre-existence view of man's soul/spirit, except the eternal Christ, as God, pre-existed before He took on His flesh (see Christology). *I believe in the miraculous giving of a new life or spirit at birth. However, I don't believe a spirit is being passed on at birth because that presupposes a parent passes on the material and is also creating the immaterial, which I believe God uniquely creates.*

Final State of Man
Where are we going? What is our destiny? God says that mortal man will take on immortality (**1Co. 15:53-54**) to one of two places. God gives an eternal choice to be with Him in Heaven, or without Him in Hell. What do you choose today? None of us is promised tomorrow...see Soteriology.

Missing the mark; falling short; losing our trust; proudly dying; guilty pleasures; leaving our love; missing intimacy; needing security; what can I do?

Introduction

Hamartiology comes from the Greek stems *"Hamartano"*, meaning sin, and *"logos"*, meaning a word about, the science of, or the study of; thus **Hamartiology is the study of Sin**. Since Angels and Man are the only two accountable for sin, some do not list Hamartiology as a separate doctrine, but include it under Man and Angels, respectively. Some key verses are **Rom. 3:23**, **5:12**, and **6:23**. **Rom. 3:23** says, "For all have sinned, and come short of the glory of God;" **Rom. 5:12** says, "Wherefore, as by one man sin entered into the world, and death by sin; and So death passed upon all men, for that all have sinned." **Rom. 6:23** says, "For the wages of sin *is* death; but the gift of God *is* eternal life through Jesus Christ our Lord."

Definition

Sin is broadly defined as rebellion or rejection of God, His rule, ways, or law; missing the mark (the mark is God and His perfections or glory). It is breaking God's revealed law (which reflects Him and His character), not trusting or believing God (**Rom. 14:23** says, "whatsoever is not of faith is sin"). If in doubt, leave it out. Sin stems from pridefully choosing to trust, love, or worship self, someone, or something above, or other than God.

Hebrew words defining sin include: 1) chata' {*khaw-taw'*}, chata'ah {*khat-aw-aw'*}, chatta'ah {*khat-taw-aw'*} or chatta'th {*khat-tawth'*}: "sin, miss the mark"; 2) 'ashmah {*ash-maw'*}: "sin, guilt, trespass"; 3) 'asham {*aw-shawm'*}: "sin, guilt, trespass, offense"; 4) shagah {*shaw-gaw'*}: "sin, err, go astray, deceived"; and 5) `avon {*aw-vone'*} or `avown {*aw-vone'*}: "sin, iniquity, depravity".

Greek words defining sin include: 1) hamartia {*ham-ar-tee'-ah*}: "sin, err, miss the mark, offend, trespass"; 2) hamartema {*ham-ar'-tay-*}

mah}: "sin, evil deed"; and 3) hamartano: {ham-ar-tan-o'}: "sin, to err, to miss the mark, or deviate from God's will or law".

Origin

The first regarded sin was committed by **Satan (Isa. 14:12 - 17; Eze. 28:12 - 19)**—**Isa. 14:12 - 15** says, "How art thou fallen from heaven, O Lucifer, son of the morning! How art thou cut down to the ground, which didst weaken the nations! For thou hast said in thine heart, I will ascend into heaven, I will exalt my throne above the stars of God: I will sit also upon the mount of the congregation, in the sides of the north: I will ascend above the heights of the clouds; I will be like the most High. Yet thou shalt be brought down to hell, to the sides of the pit." **Eze. 28:12 - 19** says, "Son of man, take up a lamentation upon the king of Tyrus, and say unto him, Thus saith the Lord GOD; Thou sealest up the sum, full of wisdom, and perfect in beauty. Thou hast been in Eden the garden of God; every precious stone was thy covering, the sardius, topaz, and the diamond, the beryl, the onyx, and the jasper, the sapphire, the emerald, and the carbuncle, and gold: the workmanship of thy tabrets and of thy pipes was prepared in thee in the day that thou wast created. Thou art the anointed cherub that covereth; and I have set thee so: thou wast upon the holy mountain of God; thou hast walked up and down in the midst of the stones of fire. Thou wast perfect in thy ways from the day that thou wast created, till iniquity was found in thee. By the multitude of thy merchandise they have filled the midst of thee with violence, and thou hast sinned: therefore I will cast thee as profane out of the mountain of God: and I will destroy thee, O covering cherub, from the midst of the stones of fire. Thine heart was lifted up because of thy beauty, thou hast corrupted thy wisdom by reason of thy brightness: I will cast thee to the ground, I will lay thee before kings, that they may behold thee. Thou hast defiled thy sanctuaries by the multitude of thine iniquities, by the iniquity of thy traffic; therefore will I bring forth a fire from the midst of thee, it shall devour thee, and I will bring thee to ashes upon the earth in the sight of all them that behold thee. All they that know thee among the people shall be astonished at thee: thou shalt be a terror, and never shalt thou be any more." *The Isaiah passage discusses earthly* *kingdoms and their evil rulers and the fall of Satan ("Lucifer"). He shows the five prideful "I will" statements and Satan's ultimate end in Hell for all to see his judgment. In the Ezekiel passage, God again discusses this wicked inspired earthly king and discusses the creation, state, role, location, and fall of Satan ("Cherub"). God says Lucifer was beautiful, wise, bright, covered with beautiful jewels and music. Satan was in heaven ("the holy mountain of God" and the Garden of Eden), anointed and covered (most assume an honor protecting others from God's consuming holiness and glory. Then, he chose to violently iniquitously greatly sin and profane the consecrated place; so, God shows six judgment "I will" statements that cause Satan to be cast down to the earth ("the ground") before man. Ultimately Satan will be completely destroyed.*

The second recorded sin was committed by **Fallen Angels (Rev. 12:1-14)**—**Rev. 12:4** says, "And his tail drew the third part of the stars of heaven, and did cast them to the earth." One third of all elect angels chose to sin and follow Satan (described in **Revelation 12** as a Great Red Dragon pulling down angels with his tail, which resulted in many red horned and dragon tailed images of the Devil) and the elect angels who chose to become fallen angels, <u>demons</u>, or <u>non-elect angels</u> (see Angelology), who were also cast to earth with Satan (**Rev. 12:9, 10, 12, 13**).

The third recorded sin was committed by **Man** or Adam (**Gen. 2:16-17; 3:6**)—"And the LORD God commanded the man, saying, 'Of every tree of the garden thou mayest freely eat: But of the tree of the knowledge of good and evil, thou shalt not eat of it: for in the day that thou eatest thereof thou shalt surely die.'" *Only one law, command, or prohibition given to Adam, which Adam gave to Eve, but they both chose to sin against God's one and only law.* **Gen. 3:6** says, "And when the woman saw that the tree was good for food, and that it was pleasant to the eyes, and a tree to be desired to make one wise, she took of the fruit thereof, and did eat, and gave also unto her husband with her; and he did eat." *Both Adam and Eve chose to sin against God.*

Next, was all **Mankind** (**Rom. 3:23; 5:12; 3:10 - 19**). **Rom. 3:23**—"For all have sinned, and come short of the glory of God." **Rom. 5:12**—"Wherefore, as by one man sin entered into the world, and death by sin; and so death passed upon all men, for that all have sinned." **Rom. 3:10 - 19**—"As it is written, There is none righteous, no, not one: There is none that understandeth, there is none that seeketh after God. They are all gone out of the way, they are together become unprofitable; there is none that doeth good, no, not one. Their throat is an open sepulcher; with their tongues they have used deceit; the poison of asps is under their lips: Whose mouth is full of cursing and bitterness: Their feet are swift to shed blood: Destruction and misery are in their ways: And the way of peace have they not known: There is no fear of God before their eyes. Now we know that what things soever the law saith, it saith to them who are under the law: that every mouth may be stopped, and all the world may become guilty before God." See also **1Ki. 8:46**; **2Ch. 6:36**; **Psa. 14:3**; **53:3**; **Ecc. 7:20**; **Gal. 3:22**.

Many speak of **Original Sin**. It is defined as the 1st sin by the 1st man (Adam) committed in the garden, which results in death and depravity for all mankind. *Although Satan, Fallen Angels, and Eve first sinned, most theologians credit Adam's sin as the Original sin (of mankind), or the condition that brought death (and many say sin) to all mankind (cf. **Romans 5:12-19**).*

Transmission of Sin
Distilled below are <u>three main views of how sin is transmitted.</u>

(1) **Seminal (Seed)**—Sin is passed down to children through their father's sperm or seed (ultimately unbroken seed descending from Adam). Man becomes a sinner by having a human father (Augustinian view). This view states that Jesus was sinless, as He was without an earthly father or seed (only earthly mother and seed directly from the Holy Spirit). This view frequently cites verses like **Deu. 5:9**, which says, ". . . God, visiting the iniquity of the fathers upon the children unto the third and fourth generation of them that hate me," and even though there is a comma there, they frequently

do not quote, **Deu 5:10** which says, "And shewing mercy unto thousands of them that love me and keep my commandments." And they certainly do not quote **Deu. 24:16**, which says, "The fathers shall not be put to death for the children, neither shall the children be put to death for the fathers: every man shall be put to death for his own sin." *Sin requires death, and God states in His law that others shall not be put to death for someone else's sin. I believe God is patient and merciful to all generations and that He does NOT hold me accountable for Adam's sin, only my own sin. I do believe the seed of man has become physically weakened by sin's consequences, but do not believe that sin is passed down through physical sperm. I have seen actions of family and friends mentored and mimicked (chosen) and handed down from generation to generation as a result. As well, I have seen children pay a heavy price from the sins of fathers and others, as we all do by the sins of those around. Abusive or alcoholic fathers frequently (by choice) have children that learn and repeat those sins to the third and fourth generations.*

(2) **Federal Headship (Representative)**—When Adam sinned, he represented all mankind. Those who ascribe to this view believe that man becomes a sinner by having Adam as the representative head. Furthermore, those holding this view believe that Jesus was His own representative, and therefore he didn't sin, and thus was sinless. *I do believe that Adam did represent mankind and insured that all would die and become sinners; however, I do not concur that he transmitted his sin to me. I believe the perfect (innocent and sinless) man (Adam), created by and walking with the perfect Creator (God), with the perfect woman (Eve), in the perfect environment (God's garden without any sin, sickness, sorrow, or death), with only one law (don't eat of the Tree of the Knowledge of Good and Evil), still CHOSE to distrust God and sin—thus commencing sin, sickness, death, and the curse upon creation, woman, and man. This best case scenario failed, and clearly shows and insures that all descending mankind (in sinful scenarios) will also indeed sin.*

(3) **Individual/Personal (Rom. 5:12)**—Everyone becomes a sinner, when they choose to sin and "His own iniquities shall take the wicked

himself, and he shall be holden with the cords of his sins" (**Pro. 5:22**). All will, and have chosen to sin (**Rom. 3:23**). This view states Jesus never chose to sin, thus was sinless (see Christology, especially Peccability views). *I believe this is how everyone becomes a sinner. God doesn't make you or me a sinner because someone else sinned; that would not be a just or fair of God. We become sinners because we choose to sin.*

Imputation Views

This is closely related to transmission, slightly different, but frequently it is coupled with one of the transmission views. <u>When does one become a sinner</u>? When is sin ascribed, attributed, or imputed? When does a person become accountable for sin, or what is the "Age of Accountability"? There are five main views:

(1) **Adam's Sin (Rom. 5:14 - 19)**—"Nevertheless death reigned from Adam to Moses, even over them that had not sinned after the similitude of Adam's transgression, who is the figure of him that was to come. But not as the offence, so also is the free gift. For if <u>through the offence of one many be dead</u>, <u>much more the grace of God, and the gift by grace, which is by one man, Jesus Christ, hath abounded unto many</u>. And not as it was by <u>one that sinned, so is the gift</u>: for the <u>judgment was by one to condemnation, but the free gift is of many offences unto justification</u>. For if <u>by one man's offence death reigned by one; much more they which receive abundance of grace and of the gift of righteousness shall reign in life by one, Jesus Christ</u>.) Therefore, as <u>by the offence of one judgment came upon all men to condemnation</u>; even so <u>by the righteousness of one the free gift came upon all men unto justification of life</u>. For as <u>by one man's disobedience many were made sinners</u>, so <u>by the obedience of one shall many be made righteous</u>." For further clarification see **Rom. 5:12** on View 4; Federal, Augustinian, or Seminal Views are the most popular. This traditional Calvinistic view states that Adam's sin caused all man to be accountable for Adam's sin and all are immediately depraved. However, the above Scripture repeats several times that due to Adam's sin <u>that resulted in death (not sin)</u> when it states that the "offence" and "disobedience" of one (Adam)

brings death, condemnation, and sin (**Rom. 5:17-19**). This view holds that this is universalism of sin to all mankind. The opposition states that forcing that view also requires universalism of salvation to all mankind by complimentary phrases like "much more they which receive abundance of grace and of the gift of righteousness shall reign in life by one, Jesus Christ" and "even so by the righteousness of one the free gift came upon all men unto justification of life" and "so by the obedience of one shall many be made righteous," where all mainstream views do not hold double universalism (or both transmitted sin and salvation). *I believe just as one clearly has to personally appropriate Jesus' death, burial, and resurrection righteousness by faith alone to be saved, or you are NOT saved; likewise, one must appropriate Adam's sin by personally sinning.*

(2) **Conception (Psa. 51:5)**—"Behold, I was shapen in iniquity; and in sin did my mother conceive me." This view explains that sin/iniquity is imputed at conception. However, opponents state that this doesn't refer to imputation, but rather refers to the sinful unwed sexual act that resulted in his conception. *This verse is also a central verse demonstrating life and accountability (which begins at conception) for the sin of abortion.*

(3) **Birth**—This view maintains that one can't sin before birth; therefore, sin is imputed at birth. **John 9:1-3** says, "And as Jesus passed by, he saw a man which was blind from his birth. And his disciples asked him, saying, Master, who did sin, this man, or his parents, that he was born blind? Jesus answered, Neither hath this man sinned, nor his parents: but that the works of God should be made manifest in him." *This view is not as popular as the conception view, since there are no specific Scriptures; as you can see, even the disciples thought this was the case; that he was "born in sin".*

(4) **1ˢᵗ Individual/Personal Sin (Rom. 5:12)**—"Wherefore, as by one man sin entered into the world, and death by sin; and so death passed upon all men, for that all have sinned" This Pelagian, or Arminian view explains this verse says that Adam had the first sin of man, which resulted in death (not sin to all men). It says so death

(not sin) "passed upon all man" and provides the reason, "for all have sinned", not "for Adam sinned". This states that each man's sin produces his own death (cf. **Rom. 6:23**) after Adam's example, not that each individual sinned "in Adam". *This view is very compelling as it holds each person accountable once they sin.*

(5) **1ˢᵗ Understanding of Law** (cf. **Rom. 5:13**)—"For until the law sin was in the world: but sin is not imputed when there is no law." This verse actually refers to the Law that was received by Moses; but many do state that UNTIL a child understands God's moral law (could be by family, peers, government, or society) or revealed Mosaic Law, has a conscience and chooses to violate it, sin is not imputed. *This is frequently an important part of an "Age of Accountability" tenet. A young child or mentally handicapped person may sin, but not fully understand, so is not as culpable or accountable. Incidentally this is even supported by American law. **2Sa. 12:16-23** provides a picture of a newborn baby that dies and David says, "I shall go unto him, but he shall not return to me." Many state this is a recognition that this child shall be in heaven with David although the child wasn't old enough to understand or have sin imputed to them, or yet to trust or reject God. This view is quite compelling as even fallen parents don't ascribe/impute sin to a baby usually until the baby understands a "law" that has been given and consciously disobeyed. Most parents can see it in their child's eyes, and this is normally when parents begin punishment and discipline. God certainly operates more lovingly and fairly than man. This view does not allow a person without enough mental maturity to "Blaspheme the Spirit" (see Pneumatology).*

<u>Position Under Sin—Total Depravity</u>
We are totally depraved, not just not perfect or sick—"dead in trespasses and sins", "children of disobedience", "children of wrath", "dead in sins", and "dead in your sins" (**Eph. 2:1-3, 5; Col. 2:13**). The word depravity is not found in Bible, but the concept is. Depravity means morally corrupt or bankrupt in character, resulting in depraved works or actions. Since the fall, or at least the imputation of sin to man (regardless of view), all believe man has been

depraved. Many speak of the "image of God in man" was defaced, but not erased. Our position since sin is one of moral bankruptcy apart from the work of Christ. Even our good or best works, "all our righteousnesses are as filthy rags" (**Isa. 64:6**). Every false religion and cult state that you can do good to get to God. This is patently false. *The most important truth for an unsaved person to understand is that they are not good, but depraved, hopelessly lost, in need of a Savior.*

Types of Sin

Sin of Commission (Rom. 3:23)—Doing wrong, committing wrong, sin; "all have sinned". **Sin of Omission (Rom. 3:23)**—Not doing right, or the best; not bringing God the greatest glory; omitting doing what

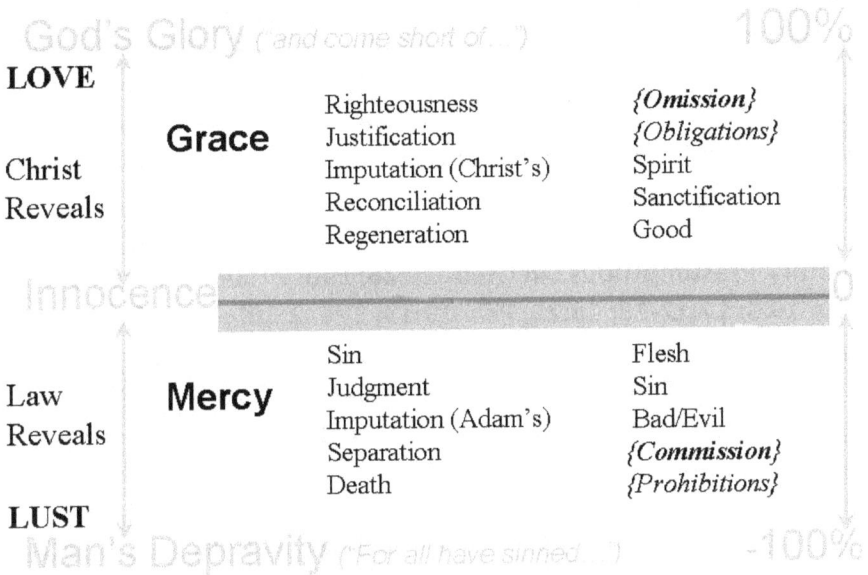

God's Glory (and come short of...)   100%

LOVE			
		Righteousness	*{Omission}*
	Grace	Justification	*{Obligations}*
Christ		Imputation (Christ's)	Spirit
Reveals		Reconciliation	Sanctification
		Regeneration	Good

Innocence

		Sin	Flesh
Law	**Mercy**	Judgment	Sin
Reveals		Imputation (Adam's)	Bad/Evil
		Separation	*{Commission}*
		Death	*{Prohibitions}*
LUST			

Man's Depravity ("For all have sinned...")   -100%

is right; "and come short of the glory of God". *See **Romans 3:23** chart below showing commission/omission. Though many do not consider Omission a sin (but omission of good or best), it is definitely falling short of God's glory or perfections. Through faith in Christ we have imputed the righteousness or perfections of God! In view of our spiritual heritage let's not just refrain from sin and still live in the gray or amoral), let's choose highest good, the best.*

Venial versus Mortal Sin—These types of sin are defined by Roman Catholicism, but they are not specifically stated in the Bible. Basically, a venial sin isn't as immoral as a mortal sin. Catholics state that venial sins still allow love to exist in us and can be mitigated by acts of love. Catholics define a mortal sin as much more serious; it is willful, leads to spiritual death, and requires conversion back to God through what is called the Sacrament of Confession. *See Biblically stated sin categories of Ignorance or Presumption below, which have some similarities, but not loss of salvation.*

Sin of Ignorance (Lev. 4:2, 13, 22, 27; 5:15, 18; Num. 15:24-29; cf. Acts 17:30; Eph. 4:18; 1Pe. 1:14; 2Pe. 2:15)—A sin that someone accidently commits who didn't know or understand it was a sin when they did it. American law would say that "ignorance is no excuse," because it is still evil, although frequently there is a reduced penalty. The Bible indicates clearly a responsibility for this sin, once it is known. It even indicates that the nation or community around that individual has a responsibility for that sin, even when unknown, but especially when known.

Willful / Presumptuous Sin (Heb. 10:26; Exo. 21:14; Num. 15:30; Deu. 1:43; 17:12-13; 18:22; Psa. 19:13; 2Pe. 2:10)—Sins that someone consciously and willfully chooses after clearly understanding them to be sinful, or wrong. Frequently, arrogance and anger characterize self-willed, presumptuous sins. Both the saved and unsaved sin willfully and presumptuously. Thankfully, the saved can confess and be cleansed to restore fellowship with God (**1Jo. 1:9**). **Hebrews 10:26** says, "For if we sin willfully after that we have received the knowledge of the truth, there remaineth no more sacrifice for sins". *I believe this verse is clearly not talking about "losing salvation," or a sin a Christian can commit (see Soteriology). If an unsaved person rejects Jesus (the only Lamb of God and true and final Sacrifice able to take away any and all sins), "there remaineth no more sacrifice for sins". I believe the Bible does show these as "worse" sins than sins of ignorance, but any sin is a sin, regardless of the degree of evil. Even our American law recognizes that concept in* *degree of murder (1ˢᵗ, 2ⁿᵈ...), as premeditated, understood, and intentional in the type of sentence imposed.*

7 Deadly or **Abominable Sins** (**Pro. 6:16-19**)—"These six things doth the LORD hate: yea, seven are an abomination unto him:" (1) "A proud look," (Pride: Eyes); (2) "A lying tongue, and" (Lying: Tongue); (3) "Hands that shed innocent blood," (Violence: Hands); (4) "An heart that deviseth wicked imaginations," (Idolatry / Wicked Plotting: Heart / Mind); (5) "Feet that be swift in running to mischief," (Quick to Evil/Mischievous: Feet); (6) "A false witness that speaketh lies, and " (False Witness/Liar: Tongue); and (7) "He that soweth discord among brethren." (Troublemaker/Discord: Hands/Tongue).

The Unpardonable Sin—the only sin that will not be forgiven by God is the **Blasphemy of the Holy Spirit** (*see Pneumatology for detailed views*).

"A Sin Unto Death" versus **"A Sin Not Unto Death"** (**1Jo. 5:15-18**)— "A sin not unto death" is listed specifically twice in Bible, **1Jo. 5:16, 17** and is any sin from which a person does not soon die, (although any sin leads ultimately to death; **Rom. 6:23**). How do you know if it is a "sin not unto death"? Simply, if a person does not soon die. "A sin unto death" (listed specifically once in Bible, **1Jo. 5:16**) is one of specific sins, a fatal sin that immediately leads to physical death (e.g. suicide). Some say it is the last or final sin (could be any "normal" sin) that leads to physical death (the last sin in the hardening process of rejecting the Holy Spirit's leading and God's chastening; the one that God knows is the last one; the point of no return, maybe even a sin for which a believer would not repent, or a sin so destructive to their testimony that God mercifully brings them home to heaven). Death, mercifully, could prevent worse sins. Possibly when the consequences of a believer's sin will be so devastating, or continued (cf. **James 5:20** "hide a multitude of sins") that God in His mercy allows Satan to destroy their flesh (but not spirit, cf. **1Co. 5:5**; allows a mercy-killing, for him and/or others, resulting from love). This may be another reason why He says, "I do not say that he shall pray for it." In these cases, it is not as loving to permit a child to continue to suffer, or cause others to suffer due to severity of sin. All sin leads to death but not at the same rapidity. We often see that some suffer more swiftly than others. These clearly refer to sins of a saved person (**1Jo. 5:16**) as we "see his brother sin", 51 times in 1 John where he uses "love", "loveth", or "beloved", 35 times "son", "sons", or "children", 13 times "brother" or "brother's." These are in the context of a believer's fellowship, forgiveness, and assurance. The proof of this context is seen in the use of "we" in every verse, and the fact that John had already said in **1Jo. 3:14**, "We know that we have passed from death unto life" (spiritually), and **1Jo. 5:13** says you "may know that you have eternal life" (spiritually). Suicide, fatal sinfully acquired sickness/venereal disease, possibly capital crime/sin (cf. **Ezra 7:26**) are clear examples of "sin unto death." **Eze. 3:20-21** (cf. **18:20-32**)—A sinner dies in sin, and if we don't warn sinners, we're guilty of their death. **Psa. 19:13** (cf. **Num. 15:30**; **Deu. 17:12-13**)—is a prayer to deliver from presumptuous sins/the great transgression (a sin unto death). **Pro. 11:19**—pursue evil to your own death. **Pro. 13:14**—depart from snares of death. **Pro. 19:16**—those despising obedience shall die. **1Co. 5:1-6**—prideful fornication led to physical body delivered to Satan, but the spirit was saved. **1Co. 11:26-30**—taking the Lord's Supper unworthily caused physical death ("sleep" a euphemism for death). **Acts 5:1-11**—lied to God and died (unsure whether saved or not). **Psa. 118:18**—discipline me not unto death (believe from King David). **James 5:13-20**—faithful prayer with confession can save a person from death and hide many sins.

Penalty or Result of Sin

The immediate result or penalty of sin is **guilt**, or a **convicted conscience** (**Rom. 2:15**; **3:19**; **James 2:10**). This causes many other fears, anger, insecurities, doubt, worry, blame, and other psychological defense mechanisms. All sin ultimately results in **death** (**Rom. 6:23**). **Physical death**—Many disparate definitions have existed over the past few decades as science matures (Science has defined death as breathing and/or heart stopped. This was later changed to add timeframes for both, and later defined as the cessation of brain activity, and probably will continue to change as our medical profession matures). <u>Physical death is the separation of the body from a relationship with the spirit; the separation of the material from the immaterial</u>. This occurs once at physical death, (**Heb. 9:27**) unless God miraculously intervenes as seen a few times in Scripture where God raised someone from the dead (e.g. **Joh. 11:44**). Some governments execute capital punishment for certain sins or broken laws (e.g. premeditated murder). **Spiritual death—** <u>the separation of one's spirit from a relationship with God</u>; <u>the separation of man's spirit from God's Spirit</u>. This spiritual death is temporary if one is "born again" or one's spirit is raised to spiritual life as one becomes a Christian. **Eternal spiritual death** is <u>eternal separation from a relationship with God forever</u>, both <u>separation of one's material and immaterial from God eternally</u>.

Remedy for Sin

Faith in Jesus Christ (Joh. 3:16; 1Jo. 5:4, 5; etc.) is the only eternal remedy for sin. One's spiritual death ends by receiving Christ's payment for sin by Christ's taking their death upon Himself. A Christian can have spiritual intimacy and fellowship by **Confession** or **Repentance (1Jo. 1:9)**—"If we confess our sins, He is faithful and just to forgive us our sins, and to cleanse us from all unrighteousness." Sometimes confession is called the "Christian bar of soap." *See Soteriology for detailed definitions of confession and repentance.*

Overcoming Temptation

God promises and provides an escape (1Co. 10:13) for each temptation—"There hath no temptation taken you but such as is common to man: but God is faithful, who will not suffer you to be tempted above that ye are able; but will with the temptation also make a way to escape, that ye may be able to bear it." **God rewards His children as they endure temptations**. He doesn't tempt (**James 1:12-15**)—"Blessed is the man that endureth temptation: for when he is tried, he shall receive the crown of life, which the Lord hath promised to them that love him. Let no man say when he is tempted, I am tempted of God: for God cannot be tempted with evil, neither tempteth he any man: But every man is tempted, when he is drawn away of his own lust, and enticed. Then when **lust** hath conceived, it bringeth forth <u>sin</u>: and sin, when it is finished, bringeth forth **death**." The logical progression of yielding to temptation is called the LSD of the Bible (Lust, Sin, and Death). **Flee lusts and temptation (1Co. 6:18; 10:12-14; 1Ti. 6:11; 2Ti. 2:22)**—A wise person realizes that they aren't strong enough to face their fleshly lusts and demons and stays away from trouble. A strong spiritual **walk with God for victory over sin** and the lusts of our flesh is only found for a Christian by "living" and "**walking in the Spirit**" (**Gal. 5:16, 25; Eph. 5:18; Rom. 8:14**), **putting on the full armor of God (Eph. 6:10-18), depending on God's Word (Psa. 119:9-11), aligning our will with God in prayer (1Th. 5:17; Mat. 6:10; Luk. 11:2),** and **putting up walls to protect the weakness of our flesh**, such as accountability partners (*see Pneumatology*). You always win when you choose NOT to sin.

So great a salvation / Savior; God's grace is sufficient, and all I need forever; let love, eternal security, and abundant life begin now.

Introduction

Soteriology comes from the Greek stems *"Soteria"*, meaning salvation, save, saving, safety, deliverance, health, or rescue, and *"logos"*, meaning a word about, the science of, or the study of; thus **Soteriology is the study of Salvation.** Some key verses are **Joh. 3:16** and **Eph. 2:8-9. Joh. 3:16** says, "For God so loved the world, that He gave His only begotten Son, that whosoever believeth in Him should not perish, but have everlasting life." **Eph. 2:8-9** says, "For by grace are ye saved through faith; and that not of yourselves: it is the gift of God; not of works, lest any man should boast."

Definitions

Salvation is a broad term, includes both eternal and temporal salvation. **Temporal/Earthly:** In the temporary sense, salvation means that a person is saved from physical or spiritual consequences of sin or a negative event. Normally, this saving from negative consequences is choosing God's right way, but can be merely being saved from anything perceived as negative. These consequences include: guilt, damaged reputation, embarrassment, seared conscience, legal or parental reprisal, physical pain, sickness, death, fire, flood, increased opportunity or temptation for more sin, loss of rewards, God's discipline or training, etc. Temporal or earthly salvation can be gained by the ongoing daily choices of obedience to God's Word and His Spirit's leading or maybe just circumstantial or personal generosity of others. These many ongoing rescues or salvations may occur for both the saved and unsaved. This is described here as most people see the word saved or salvation and automatically wrongfully interpret it to mean eternal salvation. Frequently in Scripture, when "saved" or "salvation" is not referring to eternal salvation, it is normally describing an event or explaining how a person can be saved or delivered from something negative. This can be very confusing if someone tries to add extra works or conditions to eternal salvation, based on a command or invocation for a temporary or earthly salvation.

Eternal/Heavenly: In the eternal sense, a person is eternally saved from sin and its consequence, ultimately physical and spiritual death, or Hell (cf. **Rom. 6:23**). Jesus died, was buried, and rose again to pay the eternal consequence of sin, and offers eternal salvation (heaven, life everlasting) to all who believe in Him (cf. **Joh. 3:15-18, 36; 6:29, 40, 47; 11:25-26; 1Co. 15:3-4**). Eternal or heavenly salvation is a one-time gift received by grace, through faith (**Eph. 2:8-9**). Salvation has a very simple and basic **requirement, Faith, and faith alone!** "For by grace are you **saved through faith** . . ." (**Eph. 2:8**).

Faith defined: True faith involves the entire person (Intellect, Emotions, and Will). It is NOT just knowledge of **what Christ did for us**—that is history. It is NOT just an **emotional feeling**—that is guilt or conviction. It is NOT just **choosing to say "I believe"**—that may, in fact, be lying. Personal faith believes what Jesus has accomplished, while having a heart felt conviction of sin, (*repentance), and by an act of the will, chooses to receive the free gift that God offers. One then who truly believes, is placing their total faith and trust in Christ ALONE for salvation. This believer, realizing what has been accomplished for them, should thank Jesus and want to live a life pleasing to God—not to be saved, but because they have been saved, and now for the first time have the ability to do so.

Repentance defined: Isn't repentance another condition or requirement, or is it the same as faith? Greek *"metanoia"* - reversal of another's decision, to think differently, reconsider, a change in mind or direction, to care afterwards, regret (cf. **2Co. 7:9-11**). Faith and repentance are not identical, but faith and repentance are inseparable. They are intertwined so that true faith includes repentance as one act, not two separate conditions to be saved. Turning from something to something, can be two separate acts (e.g. "turning from sin to God"). However, turning to something from something is one act (e.g. "turning to God from sin"). When you turn to something, you have to turn away from something, it is impossible not to. Invariably, in turning to God, one always turns away from sin.

Biblical, eternal salving repentance is seen in **1Th. 1:9**, where God says the Thessalonians "turned to God, from idols." Also, Paul says in **Acts 20:21**; he was testifying "repentance towards God, and faith toward our Lord Jesus Christ." The direction of eternal salvific repentance is toward God (cf. **Acts 9:35; 15:19; 2Cor. 3:16**); for if you turn to something, you are always turning from something. This sounds like a fruitless discussion in semantics, but it is not. There is one, and only one condition for salvation and that is true belief. In salvation, the believer is not just turning from sin to God; it is not just not believing in sin, but believing in God); it is turning to God from sin! Similarly, receiving is inseparable from believing. God offers a free gift—you ask (receive) by faith! If you believe, you receive.

Confession defined: Confession (Greek *homologeo* - to say the same thing, *"homo"*- the same, Greek *"logos"* - a word about, the science of). Thus, confession is to say, or admit the same thing that God says. It is seeing Jesus Christ and our sin in the same way God does. What about confession with your mouth described in **Rom. 10:9-10**? "That if thou shalt confess with thy mouth the Lord Jesus, and shalt believe in thine heart that God hath raised him from the dead, thou shalt be saved. For with the heart man believeth unto righteousness; and with the mouth confession is made unto salvation." This of course, can be applied for all. However, **Romans 9-11** is a parenthetical section about God's sovereign plan for the nation of Israel. This is a requirement for the nation of Israel to be saved (who openly put Christ to death confessing, "Crucify Him, crucify Him") and must openly confess Jesus for their national restoration and "times of refreshing." The word "confess" in its varying forms occurs only 44 times in the whole Bible, twenty times in the OT and 24 times in the NT. Several of those times are repetitive, quoting of the same statement. Very few, if any of these times are addressing eternal salvation as the result of confession. However, confession is indeed involved in eternal salvation. Obviously one must agree with God in the facts of being a sinner and that Christ was the One who paid for sin, and then simply by faith receive what He has accomplished. This type of confession is again inseparable from true belief, which also entails true repentance. If by confession, one means to verbally tell other(s) what God or we have done, or getting up before a certain number of people to tell them something, then obviously this has nothing to do with obtaining eternal salvation. A person when hearing and accepting the gospel would naturally feel compelled to verbally tell someone, if not everyone, if they truly believe the great news. Thus "if thou shalt confess with thy mouth the Lord Jesus," is a way of producing earthly or temporal salvation, making a stand, enabling confirmation of what has happened, and will certainly be a result of having been eternally saved—a person won't be able to not "confess" in many ways. Certainly those unable to speak will confess in many ways, other than verbally. See water baptism below as one of the greatest testimonies and opportunities to confess with our mouth that we have been saved by Jesus Christ's death, burial, and resurrection.

Water Baptism: Is *water* baptism required to be eternally saved? Water baptism is a work, not a condition for eternal salvation. It is a command for Christ after salvation, so in that since is a condition for temporal salvation. We are blessed when we obey, spanked when we do not. Water baptism is one of the two ordinances in the church (*see Pneumatology*—Spirit's Involvement with Saved and *Ecclesiology*—Ordinances). It is a post-salvific command to testify to others of the believer's identification with the death, burial, and resurrection of Christ as represented by the symbol of water baptism. Spirit baptism literally accomplishes what water baptism symbolizes. All Christians are baptized by the Spirit, simultaneously with eternal salvation (**2Co. 12:12-13**). Water baptism is commanded to take place AFTER Spirit baptism, or after eternal salvation. Baptism in its varying forms occurs 88 times in the whole Bible (KJV) and only in the NT. There are really fewer references, since many of these refer to the same event, or are repetitively quoted by a different Gospel writer. Most references are about John the Baptist's baptism or Spirit baptism, not water baptism. In fact, God's Word only records four commands about baptism and none of these refers to water baptism as a requirement for eternal salvation. One of those commands is in the active voice, to water baptize others. The other three are all passive, or acted upon ("be baptized"). One of those three commands is to those that were already saved and were already living in the power of the Holy Spirit before being water baptized (**Acts 11:44-48**); so, certainly this reference couldn't be a prerequisite of eternal salvation. When a saved person decides to trust Christ as Lord or Master (dedicate or sacrifice their life in service to Him or become His disciple), water baptism ought to bear witness to the fact that he/she has been saved and desires to follow Christ in every way. That is why the Apostle Paul, one of the greatest evangelists, says, "I thank God that I baptized none of you . . . for Christ sent me not to baptize but to preach the gospel" (**1Co. 1:14-17**). Jesus also was water baptized, and that wasn't to be saved or to wash away any sins (cf. **Mat. 3:16; Mar. 1:9; Luk. 3:21**). Clearly the baptism of Christ Jesus was obedience and identification with John's message. Also, "Jesus Himself baptized not" anyone with water (**Joh. 4:2**). Further, the Bible records the thief on the cross receiving the gift of salvation without being water baptized. (**Luk. 23:39-43**). So, obviously, the false doctrine of *baptismal regeneration* (which says a person must be water baptized to be eternally saved) is a blatant misinterpretation of Scripture and a false, works-based gospel.

Communion or **The Lord's Supper**: Is *Communion* required to be saved? "The Lord's Supper" (**1Co. 11:20**) specifically is found just once in Scripture and states, "When you come together, this is not to eat the Lord's Supper." "Communion" is found three times, all in Corinthians (**1Co. 10:16; 2Co. 6:14; 13:14**). **Exodus 12** shows how the "Passover", which later was shown as a type and precursor of Christ's death, was commanded as an "ordinance" (**Exo. 12:17, 24**). Certainly, this observance was not in any way said to be a means of receiving eternal life. It is only a remembrance of Jesus' shed blood and broken flesh on the cross. In the spiritual sense, His broken body and shed blood is the means by which we are eternally saved. Taking part in Communion physically is a symbol and reminder that we are commemorating His death. That is why **1Co. 11:24-25** says and repeats again the reason for the command to take part in Communion is "in remembrance of me," and **11:26** says that as often as we do we "do shew the Lord's death til He come." It does not say that repeatedly following this command of physically representing the spiritual realty that Jesus' one time death accomplished, in any way, has a part in our eternal salvation. It wonderfully reminds us of what Jesus did for us to eternally purchase our redemption (see Ecclesiology for more detail).

Church Membership: Is *Church Membership* required to be eternally saved? Of course not; that is never even intimated in Scripture. We automatically become members of the universal church when we are saved—as part of Christ's body, the Church. We are commanded to not forsake "the assembling of ourselves together" as part of a local church or congregation of believers (**Heb. 10:25**). NEVER is Church membership EVER mentioned as a condition to be eternally saved, and Churches have different requirements for local membership *(see Ecclesiology)*.

Lordship Salvation defined: What about *Lordship Salvation*? *Lordship Salvation* is a phrase that is normally understood to mean that you must make Christ, both Savior and Lord, in order to be eternally saved. This often means faith and obedience, or faith and a commitment to completely serve Him as two requirements to be eternally saved. This is a false doctrine. These are two separate choices, or decisions. Jesus is Lord and had to be Lord to save us! Thus, we must believe He is Lord over all, especially over sin and death; but, we are trusting in Him as Savior, to save us. Our acknowledging His Lordship in our life begins at salvation, and it is identified by many when we dedicate our lives in service to Him. Actual service to Him can't take place until eternal salvation, because all our good deeds are as "filthy rags" prior to eternal salvation (**Isa. 64:6**). We then, are new creatures with the indwelling power of the Holy Spirit in us, enabling us to successfully serve our new Lord. After we have been made acceptable, we can demonstrate our gratitude and our new position and life by service, or dedication to service. Lordship by itself normally means complete service to Him as Lord or master. Is He Lord over your life? This is obviously a command in Scripture for temporal or earthly salvation, but not a command or requirement to be eternally saved. He may or may not be accepted as your total Lord right after or seemingly at the point of eternal salvation, but must be accepted as your Savior to be eternally saved.

Making Christ Lord of your life is oftentimes confused with a requirement for salvation because there are many instances in the NT where people expressed their trust in Christ as Savior and then their dedication to serve Jesus as Lord at the precise time as their salvation. They trusted Christ (decision one), and then immediately dedicated their lives to the lordship of Christ (decision two). Places like Russia, Israel, and most Islamic countries today are similar. As you place your faith in Christ as Savior, you are forced to also choose at that time, whether or not to make Him Lord of your life. A person trusting Christ under these strained conditions usually has his/her family, friends, and government desert them. In many cases, they even may be put to death! We in America are blessed, and cursed. Another confusing factor is the offer of the millennial kingdom or salvation to national Israel. This is often combined and confused with the mysterious Church age offer of eternal salvation. These offers were being offered at the same time because Christ knew that national Israel would, and was choosing to reject Him as the prophesied Messiah to come. This latter truth is observed in a *dispensational* understanding of the gospel.

Reasons against eternal salvation requiring *Lordship Salvation*: Why would God command "brothers" or those eternally saved to dedicate their lives in service to God (**Romans 12:1-2**)? They would already have dedicated their lives at the point of salvation if dedication or Lordship were a requirement of salvation. Why does God give so many commands to follow Jesus and commands for believers to serve Him? They would already be serving Him if it were a decision they made at salvation. Why does God have to chasten believers (**Heb. 12:5-11; Pro. 3:11-12; Psa. 94:12; Job 5:17**)? Let it be further stated for those who even hold a milder form of Lordship salvation— Eternal salvation does not even require a willingness to give up the former lifestyle of sin—though true belief probably will. Eternal salvation is only receiving what Christ has done for you. For example, you wouldn't require a person that is drowning from a boating accident to state that they are willing to practice safe boating habits for the rest of their life before you would throw them a life preserver! Neither would God require such a confession. That is absurd to see God's eternal salvation and gracious gift in such a light. He offers eternal salvation to all that will trust His saving arm! Being saved from an unsafe boating accident would probably result in a person practicing safe boating procedures, but certainly is not a requirement to be saved or rescued. No works of ours are involved in eternal salvation. Receiving Christ's completed work on the cross brings an eternal relationship with God. Jesus, while declaring Himself to be the only sacrifice or "bread" that gives life says in **Joh. 6:27-29**, "Labor not for the meat which perisheth, but for that meat which endureth unto everlasting life, which the Son of Man shall give unto you; for Him has God the Father sealed. Then said they unto Him, 'What shall we do, that we might work the works of God?' Jesus answered, and said unto them, '**This is the work of God**, that ye **believe** on Him whom He has sent.'" Notice that the clear words, "work of God." God does the work in salvation. No additional work needs to be added to what Christ did for us. We have only to believe to receive. Salvation (eternal) is an event, not a process! Salvific belief (which as we have seen entails repentance and confession as defined above) happens only once.

Minimum Facts to Believe

So what minimum facts must be agreed upon or believed for one to be eternally saved? **God loves** you and created you to have an eternal relationship with Him (**Joh. 3:16**). All **have sinned** and broken that relationship causing the eternal consequences of death, Hell, and separation from God (**Rom. 3:23; 5:12; 6:23**). Jesus **Christ** (God) was the only sinless man (the God-man), and therefore was able and chose to **die**, be **buried**, and **rise again** in man's place (as a substitute to pay the price of sin that we never could). Not only did He pay for sin, but He also gave us His perfect righteousness (**2Co. 5:21; Heb. 10:10-14**). The only way one can be eternally saved is by **individually trusting** (believing and receiving) Jesus Christ and what He accomplished as Savior (**Joh. 1:12; Rom. 4:5**). *Please receive by faith and don't reject by unbelief (don't delay, put off, or blatantly reject. ". . . Believe on the Lord Jesus Christ and thou shall be saved, and your house" (Acts 16:31).*

The Scarlet Thread

One beautiful tapestry woven through Scripture is called *the scarlet thread* that shows God's majestic plan to always save man by *the precious blood of Jesus*, His Son. This thread ties together God's OT loving promises that the Messiah would come and *die* in our place, and the NT promises that look back at *this greatest act of love* and friendship by *Christ's death on the cross* (cf. **Joh. 15:13**). God's eternal plan has always been that Jesus is "*the Lamb slain* from the foundation of the world" (**Rev. 13:8**). This *scarlet thread* began with man's first sin where God provided an animal *blood sacrifice* and skins to cover Adam and Eve (**Gen. 3:21; Heb. 9:27**). It continued with Able's better *blood sacrifice* than Cain's (**Gen. 4:3-7; Heb. 9:22**). After enough sin to bring the worldwide flood, Noah found God's grace in God's ark and sacrificed *blood* and burnt offerings to God's satisfaction (**Gen. 8:20-21**). The Father of the Jews (Abraham) also offered animal *blood sacrifices* in faith and said to his son, "*God will provide himself a lamb*" (**Gen. 22:7-8**). From *the Passover Lamb's blood* of Moses applied by faith to the doorposts (**Exo. 12**) to "*the blood of the Covenant*" (**Exo. 24:7-8**), ". . . almost all things are by the law purged with blood; and *without shedding of blood is no remission*" (**Heb. 9:22**). Even a harlot, Rahab trusted God's salvation and demonstrated her faith by a literal cord of "scarlet thread" in her window (**Jos. 2:18**). OT believers trusted God's promises looking forward to *the blood of Jesus* as the blood of animals provided a covering or atonement (**Lev. 17:11**). These were temporary acts of faith waiting for the true *spotless Lamb's blood* to come. "For it is not possible that the blood of bulls and of goats should take away sins." (**Heb. 10:4**). Jesus fulfilled the OT and established the NT in *His blood* (**Heb. 10:9**) "through *the offering of the body of Jesus Christ once for all*" (**Heb. 10:10**), God "perfected forever" (**Heb. 10:14**) those trusting His final *one time sacrifice*. God is completely satisfied by those *saved by grace trusting in Christ's blood alone* (**Rom. 3:24-28; 5:9**). It is *the blood of Jesus* alone that saves, nothing more and nothing less, than *Jesus' blood* and righteousness. No one has or ever will be saved except by *Jesus' blood*, which washes a believer's black sin, so thoroughly removing it that they become white as snow. What can wash away my sin?—Nothing but *the blood of Jesus*.

Eternal Security means that "once saved, always saved," "perseverance of the saints," or "one can never lose eternal salvation". **Opponents to the eternal security of the believer** hold that a Christian can lose their eternal salvation, or that there is no eternal security. They mistakenly believe that their eternal security is based upon their own ability to keep their salvation, not God's ability. This is an outworking of a works or law mentality, just not to the cult extreme. The unsaved extreme requires condition(s) other than faith to **gain** eternal salvation. Eternal security opponents require condition(s) to **maintain** eternal salvation. Opponents cite three main arguments.

1) **Questionable passages:** Some passages seem to indicate that you can "fall away" (**Heb. 6:4-6**), or that if you "sin willfully" (**Heb. 10:26**), or if we stop believing, don't "overcome," or stop abiding in Him, we might get our name blotted out of the book of life (**Joh. 15; Rev. 2:7, 11, 17, 26; 3:5; 21:8**). This is only due to an improper understanding of the true meaning of these passages. Sadly, few of us believe we get anything for free and that we can keep a gift, no matter what. God's ways are so different than ours! All bring preconceived mental and emotional baggage to Bible study that causes one to jump to wrong conclusions and enable fears to get the better of us. Normally, just understanding to whom it is written (saved or unsaved), understanding that thousands of clear passages will not change their meaning by one or two unclear ones, and looking at the context will make clear the true meaning.

2) **Encourages or permits Christians to live in sin**: If a Christian knows they can do whatever they want without apparent or evident consequences, they will even increase their "sin that grace may abound" (**Rom. 6:1**). No, this is untrue. Knowing that a person is saved eternally allows service with a different motivation of love, not fear. We are like pigs prior to salvation and a white house cat (*excuse this illustration for those non-cat lovers*) after salvation. Pigs can't help but wallow in the mud, while house cats like to keep themselves clean. When you become a Christian, you are a "new

creation" (**2Co. 5:17**) and you can sin all you want and still go to heaven, but you won't if you're truly saved. *You just won't want to sin as much and now you have the ability, through the Spirit of God not to sin. It has all been paid for and you have already received the gift of eternal life. I do sin all I want. In fact, I sin more than I want.*

3) **Experience:** "But what about "so and so" who did all this, and now he says this, and lives this way?" God alone is their Judge, and who are we to say that he was truly saved to begin with, or that he isn't now? (cf. **1Co. 11:27-32; 1Jo. 5:15-18** ". . . a sin unto death" and **Heb. 12:5-11** on "the chastening of the Lord").

Eternal Security—Proponent Rationale

Proponents: A Christian can never lose eternal salvation, no matter what they do! Once received by grace through faith, eternal security is completely dependent upon God, and not the individual. Here are over thirty reasons the Bible says a Christian is eternally secure:

1. **God provided salvation**, not man (**2Ti. 1:9; Ti. 3:5**).
2. **God keeps salvation**, not man (**1Pe. 1:3-5; 2Ti. 1:12**).
3. "**Eternal life**" means eternal life (**Joh. 10:28**)! John 6:47 says that a believer "**has**" (present tense) "**everlasting life**." How long is eternal or everlasting? That is right, unending.
4. God says believers "**shall never perish**" and that "**no man is able to pluck them out of my Father's hand**" (**Joh. 10:28-29**). Jesus said that believers shall "**never die**" (**Joh. 11:26**) and He "**will never leave**" "**nor forsake**" believers (**Heb. 13:5**). How inclusive is NEVER and are you a part of mankind? He didn't give any caveats; therefore, we conclude a Christian is secure.
5. The **nature of salvation** is to save or rescue. If God is our Savior and saved or rescued us, then **we have been truly saved and rescued** (**Mat. 18:11; Luk. 7:50; Heb. 10:39**). If not, then we have never been saved.
6. Salvation is a "**free gift**" (**Rom. 5:15-16, 18; 6:23; 11:29**).
7. Salvation is "**by grace**" and "**not of works**" (**Rom. 11:6; Eph. 2:8-10; Tit. 3:7**).
8. Salvation is "**by faith**" alone (**Eph. 2:8-10; Rom. 3:28**).

9. Salvation is recorded as a **past tense event (Joh. 1:12-13; Rom. 6:17-18; 1Jo. 5:11; Eph. 1:13-14; Col. 1:12-14)**.
10. Salvation was provided when we were "**sinners**" (**Rom. 5:8**) and "**enemies**" of God (**Rom. 5:10; Col. 1:20-21**). How can a person get worse than that?
11. Salvation is "**incorruptible**," "**undefiled**," "**fadeth not away**," and "**reserved in heaven**" (**1Pe. 1:4f**).
12. Believers were **predestinated**, **elected**, and **called** (**Rom. 8:28-39; 11:5-7; 2Ti. 1:9-10; 1Th. 5:24; 1Pe. 1:2; Eph. 1:5, 11**).
13. Believers were **Holy Spirit** (*see Pneumatology*) **sealed** (**Eph. 1:13-14; 4:30**) and **indwelt** (**John 14:16; Rom. 8:9-11**) until the day of redemption (forever). The Holy Spirit is not going to spend eternity in Hell. The Word and the Spirit give more truth to the believer, not less. The Spirit enlightens a person to the point where they may accept Christ through believing in Him. At that point (event), they are saved.
14. **Believers names were written** (probably at the point of salvation, but maybe at the foundations of the world) **in "The Lamb's Book of Life"** (**Rev. 13:8; 21:27**) and no one's name can be blotted out of the Lamb's Book of Life, or certainly God never says any names get blotted out of it. *It is my view that "The Book of Life"* (***Php. 4:3; Rev. 3:5; 17:8; 20:12, 15; 22:19***) *had everyone's name written in it before "the foundations of the world" of all who would be conceived. A person's name gets blotted out of it if they blaspheme the Holy Spirit (see Pneumatology). It is either a different book, or The Book of Life is the book that contains all the works that a person has performed. The Lamb's Book of Life only has those names written in it of those who believed the Spirit's wooing to Christ. These are they who receive eternal life, and no one's name can be blotted out of that Book.*
15. A believer's **present position** proves it was a **one-time choice** that saved, and nothing (if maintained) might obtain eternal salvation. The following occurred (past tense) at the point of salvation and continue (present tense) to be true. Nowhere in Scripture does God say that you or anyone else can ever give up any of these, and nowhere does it say any of these will ever cease! It does say these cannot be taken and they last forever!

16. Believers are now "**in Christ**" (**1Co. 1:30; Col. 3:3**). **Rom. 8:1** says, "There is therefore **now no condemnation** to them who are in Christ Jesus."
17. Believers **are now** "Adopted," "**children of God**," "**sons**," and "**brothers**" (**1Jo. 3:2; Rom. 8:15-17; Eph. 1:5; Gal. 3:26-4:7**).
18. Believers **are now** "heirs," "**joint heirs**," and "**partakers of the inheritance**" (**Rom. 8:17; Col. 1:12; Gal. 4:7**). Believers **are now** "**spiritual**," not "natural" (**1Co. 2:14-15**).
19. Believers **are now citizens in heaven** (**Php. 3:20-21; Eph. 2:19**).
20. Believers **are now new creatures, regenerated,** "**born again**," and "**partakers of the divine nature**" which changed our nature or spirit and gave us a desire to do good (**Joh. 3:3-8; 2Co. 5:17; Tit. 3:5; 2Pe. 1:4**).
21. Believers **are now** "**justified**" or legally declared righteous; it is a change in our standing before God because of Jesus, so that it is not only now, *just-if-I'd* never sinned, but also that I have been imputed or given the complete righteousness of Christ (**Rom. 3:24; 4:25; 5:8-11**).
22. Believers **are now sinless** positionally (**1Jo. 3:9; 5:18; 2Co. 5:21**).
23. Believers **are now** "**sanctified**" or set apart and made holy. It has to do with a change in character or conduct (4 types: Pre-salvific, which occurred before salvation; Positional, which occurs simultaneously with salvation; Progressive and Permanent, which are subsequent results of salvation; **Heb. 10:10, 14; 1Pe. 1:2; 1Co. 6:11; 1Th.5:23**).
24. Believers **are now redeemed or ransomed** or bought back from sin, Satan, and death (**Mat. 20:8; 1Pe.1:18; 1Ti. 2:6; Gal. 3:13**).
25. Believers **are now reconciled** or brought back into a right relationship with God; sin has been removed (**Rom. 5:10; 2Co. 5:18-19; Eph. 2:16; Col. 1:20; Heb. 2:7**).
26. Believers **are now priests** (**1Pe. 2:9; Rev. 1:6**).
27. Believers **are now saints** (**Rom. 1:7; 1Co. 1:2; Eph. 4:12; 1Th. 3:13; Col. 1:2**).
28. Believers **are now ambassadors** (**2Co. 5:20**).
29. Believers **are now God's temple** (**1Co. 3:15-17**) and building (**1Co. 2:9; Eph. 3:20-22**).
30. Believers **are now complete** (**Col. 2:10**).

31. Believers **are now gifted members** in the Christ's body (**Rom. 12; 1Co. 12; Eph. 4; 1Pe. 4**).

Eternal Security—Proponent Select Scriptures

1. **Joh. 5:24**—". . . He that heareth my Word, and believeth on Him that sent Me, has everlasting life, and shall not come into judgment, but is passed from, death unto life."
2. **Joh. 6:36-37, 40, 44**—". . . him that cometh to Me I will in no wise cast out." ". . . have everlasting life: and I will raise him up at the last day." ". . . I will raise him up at the last day."
3. **Joh. 12:8-29**—"And I give unto them eternal life; and they shall never perish, neither shall any man pluck them out of my hand. My Father, who gave them to Me, is greater than all, and no man is able to pluck them out of My Father's hand." Are you human or part of mankind?
4. **Rom. 8:18**—"If God be for us, who can be against us?"
5. **Rom. 8:27-39**—"And He that searcheth the hearts knoweth what *is* the mind of the Spirit, because He maketh intercession for the saints according to *the will of* God. And we know that all things work together for good to them that love God, to them who are the called according to *His* purpose. For whom He did foreknow, He also did predestinate *to be* conformed to the image of His Son, that He might be the firstborn among many brethren. Moreover whom He did predestinate, them He also called: and whom He called, them He also justified: and whom He justified, them He also glorified. What shall we then say to these things? If God *be* for us, who *can be* against us? He that spared not His own Son, but delivered Him up for us all, how shall He not with Him also freely give us all things? Who shall lay anything to the charge of God's elect? *It is* God that justifieth. Who *is* he that condemneth? *It is* Christ that died, yea rather, that is risen again, who is even at the right hand of God, who also maketh intercession for us. Who shall separate us from the love of Christ? *shall* tribulation, or distress, or persecution, or famine, or nakedness, or peril, or sword? As it is written, For thy sake we are killed all the day long; we are accounted as sheep for the slaughter. Nay, in all these things we are more than conquerors

through Him that loved us. For <u>I am persuaded, that neither death, nor life, nor angels, nor principalities, nor powers, nor things present, nor things to come, Nor height, nor depth, nor any other creature, shall be able to separate us from the love of God</u>, which is in Christ Jesus our Lord."

6. **Rom. 11:7**—". . . <u>the election</u> has obtained <u>it</u> . . ."

7. **1Co. 6:9-11**—"Know ye not that the unrighteous shall not inherit the kingdom of God?" "And <u>such were</u> some of you; but <u>ye are washed</u>, but <u>ye are sanctified</u>, but <u>ye are justified</u> in the name of the Lord Jesus, and by the Spirit of our God."

8. **Col. 1:12-14**—"Giving thanks unto the Father, <u>Who has made us fit to be partakers of the inheritance of the saints</u> in light; <u>Who has delivered us from the power of darkness</u>, and <u>has translated us into the kingdom of His dear Son</u>; In Whom we have redemption through His blood, even the forgiveness of sins."

9. **Col. 2:13**—"And you . . . has <u>He made alive together with Him</u>, having forgiven you all trespasses."

10. **Col. 3:3-4**—". . . and <u>your life is hid with Christ in God</u>. When Christ, who is our life, shall appear, then <u>shall you also appear with Him in glory</u>."

11. **2Ti. 1:9-10**—"Who hath <u>saved us</u>, and <u>called <i>us</i></u> with an holy calling, <u>not according to our works</u>, but <u>according to His own purpose and grace</u>, <u>which was given us</u> in Christ Jesus <u>before the world began</u>, But is now made manifest by the appearing of our Savior Jesus Christ, who <u>hath abolished death</u>, and <u>hath brought life and immortality</u> to light through the gospel."

12. **2Ti. 1:12b**—". . . <u>He is able to keep</u> that which I have committed unto Him against that day."

13. **2Ti. 2:13**—(to saved, of course) "<u>If we believe not</u>, yet <u>He abideth faithful</u>; He cannot deny Himself."

14. **Heb. 6:17-20**—"Wherein God, willing more abundantly to show unto the <u>heirs of promise</u> the immutability of His counsel, <u>confirmed it by an oath</u>, that by two immutable things, in which <u>it was impossible for God to lie</u>, <u>we might have a strong consolation</u>, who have fled for refuge to lay hold upon the hope set before us, which hope <u>we have as an anchor of the soul, both sure and steadfast</u>."

15. **Heb. 7:25**—"Wherefore, He is able to save them (forever-NASV) to the uttermost that come unto God by Him, seeing He ever liveth to make intercession for them."
16. **Heb. 9:12**—". . . by His own blood He entered in once into the holy place, having obtained eternal redemption for us."
17. **Heb. 12:10-14**—"By which will we are sanctified through the offering of the body of Jesus Christ once for all . . . after He had offered one sacrifice for sins forever . . . For by one offering He has perfected forever them that are sanctified."
18. **1Jo. 3:1-3**—"Behold, what manner of love the Father has bestowed upon us, that we should be called the children of God . . . Beloved, now are we the children of God, and it does not yet appear what we shall be, but we know that when He shall appear, we shall be like Him . . ."
19. **1Jo. 3:14**—"We know that we have passed from death unto life . . ."

Importance

Why is this such an important issue? If we don't believe in eternal salvation or security then: (1) We call God a liar, as we doubt His Word (cf. **1Jo. 5:9-11**); (2) We say His sacrifice (His blood payment) wasn't sufficient enough; and (3) We confuse many key doctrines to follow. **Law [works]** (**Rom. 3:20-29; Gal. 2:16, 20-21; 3:11**) and **Grace [faith]** (**Tit. 3:5; Rom. 3:28; 6:14**). Are we truly saved if we are trusting Christ plus works? **Salvation and Service.** Our **positional relationship with our progressive relationship** (permanent position with intimacy of fellowship). The **Character and Nature of God.** We humanistically make Him like us (cf. **Rom. 1:23**) by taking away His perfected attributes of love, grace, mercy, etc. We can't understand many passages and miss the true meaning because we **automatically misinterpret what God said.** We have **the wrong motivation for service.** It should be love, not fear (**1Jo. 4:17-18**). We **miss the joy, comfort, hope, assurance, and confidence that God has provided** (**Rom. 5:11; Eph. 3:11-12**). We **cannot fully experience "walking in the Spirit"** (**Gal. 5:16-25**). We have no perfect love (**1Jo. 4:17-18**), no full joy (**Psa. 51:12; 1Th. 2:19; 1Jo. 1:4**), no perfect peace (**Col. 3:15**), and no pure faith (**Tit. 3:5**). We are trusting in ourselves to save us and not completely in Christ. To the degree we are trusting in our own works or ourselves, we are not trusting in Christ or in His finished work.

There may be a deeper issue. Why do you think, or feel you can lose your salvation? It may be one or more of the following: (1) You are not sure and need more study (**2Ti. 2:15**); (2) Satan has sown seeds of doubt common to all that God has promised. Refresh yourself in God's promises; (3) There is a relationship problem with God (sin). You are experiencing guilt or conviction of sin and loss of fellowship with God and other believers; (4) You possibly aren't saved. You may never have known what salvation really is, and now the Holy Spirit is drawing you to Christ. Just trust Jesus for your salvation, and rest in Him.

For how many sins did Christ die and pay? ALL. What sin or sins can a believer commit to cause them not to be saved? None. It is logically impossible! Is unbelief a sin? YES, "for whatsoever is not of faith is sin" (**Rom. 14:23**). What do you do when someone doesn't believe in eternal security? You love and accept them as you would any person, and show them what God says about salvation and then allow God to convict them. Treat them as you would anyone denying any other Scriptural doctrine, yet try to make sure that they are depending on Christ alone for salvation. They are not trusting Christ to the extent that they are trusting in themselves for salvation. And of course, pray for them.

Assurances

How do you know that you are truly saved? Do you believe in Jesus? "And this is the record that <u>God has given to us eternal life</u>, and <u>this life is in His Son</u>. He that has the Son has life; and he that has not the Son of God has not life. These things have I written unto you that believe on the name of the Son of God, <u>that ye may **know** that ye have eternal life</u>, and that you may believe on the name of the Son of God. And <u>this is the confidence that we have in Him</u>..." (**1Jo. 5:11-14**a). If you have ever put your faith in or believed in Jesus, God in His immutable Word promises you that you have been given eternal life! Further indicators or proofs by your answers to the following (*several taken from John McArthur, Jr. The Security of Salvation, Romans 5:1-11 Study Notes*).

1. Have you enjoyed fellowship with Christ and His redeemed people (**1Jo. 1:3**)?
2. Are you sensitive to your sin (**1Jo. 1:8, 10**)?
3. Does something deep within you tend to hate the world and its evil (**1Jo. 2:15**)?
4. Are you obedient to God's Word (**1Jo. 2:3-5**)?
5. Do you eagerly await the coming of Jesus Christ (**1Jo. 3:2-3**)?
6. Do you see a decreasing pattern of sin in your life (**1Jo. 3:5-6**)? If you repeatedly and unrepentantly practice sin, you were never truly saved (**1Jo. 3:8-9**).
7. Do you sacrificially love other Christians (**1Jo. 3:14, 19; 4:7-8**)? We say, "but I don't always feel saved." Also **1Jo. 3:20** says, "For if our heart condemns us, God is greater than our heart, and knoweth all things." Usually it is a relationship problem and we need to confess it (**1Jo. 1:9**), or God has forgiven you, but you haven't forgiven yourself.
8. Do you experience answered prayer (**1Jo. 3:22; 5:15**)?
9. Do you experience the inner working of the Holy Spirit (**1Jo. 3:24; 4:13; 5:10; Gal. 4:6; Rom. 8:15**)?
10. Are you led by the Spirit (**Rom. 8:14**)?
11. Does the Spirit bear witness with your spirit that you are saved or God's child (**Rom. 8:16**)?
12. Do you discern between spiritual truth and error (**1Jo. 4:1-6**)?
13. Do you believe what the Bible teaches (**1Jo. 5:1**a)?
14. Have you ever been attacked or persecuted for your love or faith in God (**Php. 1:28-29; Joh. 15:20; 1Pe. 2:21; 2Ti. 3:12**)?
15. Do you experience the chastening of God (**Heb. 12:5-11; Job 5:17; Pro. 3:11-12; Psa. 94:22**)?
16. What type of fruit do you evidence in your life (**Mat. 7:16; Gal. 5:16-25; Eph. 5:9; Pro. 10:16, 18-19, 30-31; Joh. 15:1-6**)? A good tree brings forth good fruit, a bad, bad, and a baby tree, little or none for a while.

Conclusion

Please, my friend, don't depend on yourself or your own works. "...What must I do to be saved? And they said, Believe on the Lord Jesus Christ, and thou shalt be saved" (**Acts 16:30-31**). If you have believed in Jesus, you are saved eternally and you will evidence and experience some, if not all, these assurances of your salvation in your life. *Thank you Lord, for all you have done! If it depended on me to obtain or keep salvation, I would never make it to heaven.* "But thanks be to <u>God</u> Who <u>giveth us the victory through our Lord Jesus Christ</u>" (**1Co. 15:57**).

God's created fiery, flying, and fearful stars;
possessing powerful protectors and foes;
delighters and deceivers; many ministers and messengers.

Introduction

Angelology comes from the Greek stems *"Angelos"*, meaning Angel or messenger, and *"logos"*, meaning a word about, the science of, or the study of; thus **Angelology is the study of Angels**. Some key verses are **Heb. 1:14** and **Psa. 103:20**. **Heb. 1:14** says, "Are they not all ministering spirits, sent forth to minister for them who shall be heirs of salvation?" **Psa. 103:20** says, "Bless the LORD, ye His angels, that excel in strength, that do His commandments, hearkening unto the voice of His word."

What does the Bible says about: Satan, demonic gateways, seraphim, guardian angels, possession, and the Christian's response? What does a cherub really do? Is there an angel stronger than Satan? What do angels look like? Did you know some angels have six wings, some four, some two, and some look like people? Where are angels now? Can we cast out demons today? Can animals or Christians be possessed? Did giants result from angels having sex with people? Do angels marry? Do they die? What does the Bible say is angel's food? Can angels be saved? Who is the Archangel? What percentage of all angels are good or bad? See it for yourself in the only Book with absolutely angelic answers.

Angels—Elect and Key Names

The **Elect Angels** are **good** and **holy** Angels (**1Ti. 5:21; Rev. 14:10**). Several of them are named in the Bible. An angel of God or angel of the Lord is any angel. **"The"** Angel of the Lord is a pre-incarnate appearance of Jesus Christ (*see Christology*—Theophany or Christophany). The Angel **Michael** is one of the chief princes (**Dan. 10:13**). Michael is Daniel's and Israel's prince Angel (**Dan. 10:21**). Michael is called the great prince (**Dan. 12:1**), the Archangel—leads and helps good angels (**Jude 1:9**). He contends with Satan and his demons (**Jude 1:9; Rev. 12:7**) and even carries bodies of the saved (**Luk. 16:22; Jude 1:9**). **Gabriel** helped Daniel understand and stands in the very presence of God (**Daniel 8:16; 9:21; Luk. 1:19, 26**). **The Angel of the Bottomless Pit**; **Abaddon**—Hebrew; **Apollyon**—Greek; has the Key to the Bottomless Pit (**Rev. 9:11; 20:1, 3**). He seems to be stronger than Satan as he grabs, chains, and casts Satan into a prison pit.

Types and Description

The Bible designates and describes **cherubims** (65 times, only once in the NT). It is interesting to note that a **cherub** (singular; found 30 times, all in OT) isn't a cute little naked angel with a bow and love arrows for Valentine's Day. Cherubims have four faces, four wings, have hands (**Eze. 10:6, 8, 12, 21**, etc.), and are protectors of and from God's holiness, glory, or presence (mercy). **Seraphims** (**Isaiah 6:2, 6; Rev. 4:8**) have six wings and have many eyes. They use two wings to cover their face, two to cover their feet, and two to fly. They worship God, speak, and minister at God's altar. All Angels (elect or evil) were created by God (**Heb. 1:7**).

Work and Activity

Angels are God's messengers that appear and speak to men and churches, sometimes even in dreams (**Mat. 1:20; 2:13; Rev. 1:20; 2:1, 8, 12**). They serve God (**Mat. 28:2**); they worship and praise God (**Psa. 148:2; Luk. 2:13**); they fly (**Rev. 14:6**); they don't marry (**Mat. 22:30; Mar. 12:25; Luk. 20:34-36**)*; the Law was ordained by angels (**Gal. 3:19**); they are fearful, mighty, powerful, and yet good looking (**Luk. 2:9; Rev. 10:1; 18:1, 21; 2Th. 1:7; 2Pe. 2:11; Acts 6:15**); involved in healing men (**Joh. 5:4**); given power over nature in Tribulation (**Rev. 7:1-2**); not to be worshipped (**Rev. 19:10; 22:9**); used to destroy wicked (**2Sa. 24:16; 2Ki. 19:35; 1Ch. 21:12, 15-16; 2Ch. 32:21; Mat. 13:39, 41, 49**) {one killed over 185,000}, minister to children (**Mat. 18:10**); minister to those who will be saved (**Heb. 1:14**); angels witness men's confessions and denials (**Luk. 12:8-9**); rejoice when people get saved (**Luk. 15:10**); guide, go before, strengthen, and deliver those who are saved (**Gen. 24:7, 40; Exo. 23:20; 32:34; 1Ki. 19:5f; Dan. 10:18-19; Psa. 34:7; Dan. 3:28; 6:22**);

desire to understand the gospel (**1Pe. 1:12**) {*how God could love us so*}; are involved in God's judgments (**Rev. 8:3-13; 9:1, 11-14; 14:17-19**); and minister to the churches (**Rev. 2:1, 8, 12, 18; 3:1, 7, 14**).

*Angelic Gender and Procreation?

The Bible says that angels appeared like men (**Gen. 18:2, 16, 22: 19:1**, etc.), it calls the angel Gabriel a "man", Hebrew "iysh" – "man" or "male" (**Dan. 9:21**). It says we are sometimes unaware that strangers we host are angels so evidently can look like people, although it doesn't say whether they are male or female (**Heb. 13:2**). An angel tells Zechariah about what seems to be female angels, ". . . there came out two women, and the wind was in their wings; for they had wings like the wings of a stork" (**Zec. 5:9**).

Some believe that angels cannot have sex or procreate, that they were created as a fixed number. They cite, **Mat. 22:30**, which says, "For in the resurrection they neither marry, nor are given in marriage, but are as the angels of God in heaven." It doesn't say they don't have sex or don't have the ability to procreate, it does say they do not marry, nor will Christians in heaven. Most theologians believe **Gen. 6:2** is describing the results of fallen angels ("sons of God") having sex with people ("daughters of men"). They cite that "sons of God" might mean angels in **Job 1:6** and **2:1** as Satan was among them and it was before people were created (cf. **Job 38:7**). They believe this explains the reason their children became "giants", "mighty men", and "men of renown" (**Gen. 6:4**). They also hold that this is why such evil wickedness resulted requiring the flood (**Gen. 6:5f**) and is why certain fallen angels were chained (cf. **2Pe. 2:4f; Jude 6**). I do not hold this view. First, the passage is man centric and doesn't mention angels or their judgment. Next, the context after the first sin (**Gen. 3**) is the struggle between the ungodly (Cain) and godly (Able) in **Gen. 4:1-16**, the ungodly line of Cain (**Gen. 4:17-24**) and the ungodly lineage of Seth (**Gen. 4-25-26**), and the death of them both in **Gen. 5** up to Noah and the world-wide destruction by the flood of all, but godly. Logically following, **Gen. 6** shows these two lines sinfully (cf. **Ezra 9:2**) intermingling. Obviously, the bringing back together the two genetic lines would strengthen their children.

129

Also, the Hebrew "nephyil" means "feller, bully, tyrant, or giant", not just giants. Also, only two of the 11 times "sons of God" is found in the Bible could it possibly mean fallen angels, where most clearly refer to the godly people of faith. Angels don't die (**Luk. 20:36**) and have been around since before creation of the universe (**Job 38:4-7**), so we should not underestimate their knowledge, understanding, and wisdom acquired.

Angel Flesh and Nature

Angel flesh and nature is different than man's (**Heb. 2:16**). They are said to be "a flaming fire" (**Psa. 104:4; Heb. 1:7**). Angels can change their appearance. Angels have appeared like people with hands and feet and without wings (**Heb. 13:2**). Some have two, four, or six wings and fly (**Eze. 1:6; Isa. 6:2, 6**). Some have animal faces like a lion, ox, and eagle (**Eze. 1:5-25**). Some don't have feet like men, but have brazen bull hoofs (**Eze. 1:7**). Some don't have two eyes, but have many with un-described capabilities (**Eze. 1:18**). They are able to be invisible to human eyes or appear at God's beckon and will (cf. **2Ki. 6:15-17**). We don't know if this is a special disappearing capability or whether there is a different spiritual dimension where elect and fallen angels fight all around us for our hearts, minds, or even physical well-being (see **Dan. 10:10-21**, where the Angels Gabriel and Michael are battling demons from Greece and Persia to help Daniel and answer his prayers).

Angel Food, Number, and Location

"Angels' food" is not light cake, but is manna (**Psa. 78:24-25; Exo. 16:35**—*this may have been a reference that angels distributed manna to the Israelites in the wildness*. There are more than 12 legions; they are innumerable (**Mat. 26:53; Heb. 12:22**); a *Legion = Regiment, for modern warfare that would be 300 to 3,000; so 12 = 3,600 to 36,000*. There are some angels located in heaven, some on earth, and some in between. There are 12 angels at the 12 gates in heaven (**Mat. 24:36; Mar. 12:25; Joh. 1:51; Rev. 21:12**).

Angels—Evil (Satan)

The **fallen Angels** are **evil, unholy, wicked**, or **demons** (Psa. 78:49). The most evil leader of all demons is Satan. The study of Satan is called Satanology, and it is dangerous. He is called: <u>Satan</u> (**1Ch. 21:1**), <u>Lucifer, son of the Morning</u> (**Isa. 14:12**), <u>The Devil</u> (**Rev. 20:2**), <u>Dragon</u> (**Rev. 12:7; 20:2**), <u>The Old Serpent</u> (**Rev. 12:9; 12:3; 20:2**), <u>The Evil</u> or <u>Wicked One</u> (**Mat. 13:19; 1Jo. 2:13-14; 5:18**), <u>The Prince / Ruler of this World</u> (**Mat. 4; Luk. 4; Joh. 12:31; 14:30; 16:11**), <u>The god of this Age/World</u> (**2Co. 4:4**), and <u>The Prince of Power of the Air</u> (**Eph. 2:2**). Satan was created and was once <u>the Anointed Cherub</u> (**Eze. 28**). Many believe Satan led the angelic worship and many musicians claim he is their inspiration of their rock-n-roll. Satan chose to sin against God and fall from His highly exalted position in heaven with his five prideful "I will" statements (**Isa. 14**). See Hamartiology, under Origin, for detail on Satan's Fall, and the universe's first sin.

Satan's Works

Satan leads and helps his demons (**Rev. 12:7**). He is the adversary, hater, accuser, slanderer, and deceiver (**1Ch. 21:1; Rev. 12:9-10; 20:2**). He is called Beelzebub, the prince of demons, Lord of the Flies, and Lord of the Dung Hill (**Mat. 12:24; Mar. 3:22**). Anton LaVey published a Satanic bible in 1969 (*considered dangerous reading*), that basically promotes the opposite of God's true Holy Bible. The Bible says that Satan "is transformed into an Angel of Light" (**2Co. 11:14**). He steals God's Word from men's hearts (**Mat. 13:19**), he tempts, resists, tries to sift Christians (**Zec. 3:1; Dan. 10:13; Mat. 4:3; Mar. 1:13; 1Th. 2:18; Luk. 22:31**). He possesses (**Joh. 13:2**) and is like a roaring lion, seeking whom he may devour (**1Pe. 5:8**). He is a ruler of darkness (**Eph. 6:2**). *Ever wonder why you are afraid of the dark?* He is the father of lies and blinds minds (**Joh. 8:44; 1Jo. 3:12-15; 2Co. 4:4**). He is a murderer (**Joh. 8:44; 1Jo. 3:12-15; Heb. 2:14**) and he puts non-Christians among Christians as the metaphor of sowing "tares" among "good seed" (**Mat. 13:38-39**).

Demons

Fallen Angels are called demons and their study is called Demonology. Again this is a dangerous area of study and should never be taken lightly. Some names include: <u>demons or devils</u> (**Luk. 7:33f**), <u>evil spirits</u> (**Acts 19:12-13, 15f**), <u>sons of God</u> (**Job 1, 2**), <u>foul spirits</u> (**Rev. 18:2**), <u>dumb and deaf spirits</u> (**Mar. 9:17**), and <u>seducing spirits</u> (**1Ti. 4:1**). As you can see their very names imply some of what they are, do, and their cause. Some of these demons are imprisoned, and some are free (**2Pe. 2:4; Jud 1:6-7; Eph. 6:12**). All shall be judged by Christians (**2Co. 6:3**). All are evil (**Psa. 78:49**), or they would not be fallen. The Bible says not to fellowship with or sacrifice to demons (**1Co. 10:20**), and it also talks about the cup or table of demons (**1Co. 10:21**). Both warn of the dangers of demonic rituals and hanging around those worshippers of magic spells, e.g., the friendly foolish of evil spirits including white and dark witches, warlocks, etc. The Bible mentions the habitation of demons (**Rev. 18:2**), where cities and other places have so given into demonic doctrines (**1Ti. 4:1**) that the places are places of destruction and debauchery. Demons not only believe in God, they know God and Satan are real (**Jam. 2:19**), but are happy if you do not. Demons can perform miracles (**Rev. 16:14**), *but I believe they are deceptive miracles that are temporary, harmful, or at best only remove bad things they have inflicted for more evil purposes*. Although you would think this wouldn't need to be said, Christians are forbidden to worship demons (**Rev. 9:20**), which is always associated with idolatry. The allure of power and unbelief tempts many teens and foolish to play around in that which can destroy. Hell was prepared for Satan and his demons (**Mat. 25:41**).

Demonic Possession

What about possession by Satan or his demonic spirits? There have been many men possessed and controlled by one demon (**Mat. 9:32-33; 15:22f**). There have also been many men possessed by multiple demons (**Luk. 8:30; Mat. 8:16, 28, 31, 33; Mar. 16:9; Luk. 8:2f**). Yes, even animals (pigs) have been possessed by evil spirits (**Mat. 8:31-32; Mar. 5:12**). *And yes that was the first recorded making of deviled-ham; that joke was kosher (sorry, my wife edited this out twice, but I added it back)*. Possession is horrible. I have talked with many who have experienced the demonic in the pastoral, psychological, pharmacological/drugs, sanitariums, multiple personalities, seizures, and other demonically induced misdiagnosed maladies. Although possession may give individuals supernatural ability of strength, knowledge, etc. (**Mat. 8; Acts 16**) that some have even exploited for financial gain, it harms the individual body, soul, and spirit (**Mat. 9:33; Mar. 5:5; Luk. 9:42f**). Demons can be cast out by the Spirit of God (**Mat. 8:28**). Exorcisms should never be taken lightly, or without prayer and fasting (**Mat. 17:17-21; Mar. 9:17-29**). Can Christians cast out demons today? They did in the early Church and there are many places around the world where many claim to regularly cast demons out by the blood and name of Jesus. The Apostles were given power to cast out demons, but couldn't cast all out; others have tried and have found themselves not prepared and failed in their attempts to do so (cf. **Luk. 9:1; Acts 19:12-20**). Exorcisms are not to be taken lightly. Many affirm that not only are there sins that can open up demonic footholds, strongholds, and gateways, but also some items (Ouija boards, Tarot Cards, Pentagrams, Séances, Astrology, etc.) and places that can do the same (**Deu. 18:10; cf. Acts 19:19; Rev. 18:2**). There are no "innocent" games that claim to play around with the supernatural. A Christian cannot be demon possessed since they have the Spirit of God indwelling, sealing, and protecting them (*see Pneumatology*) and the Holy Spirit will not tolerate that division (c.f. **Luk. 11:17**). I've seen Christians that have stumbled and are slow to get up from sin allow themselves to be demonically and spiritually oppressed, and oftentimes physically ineffective. Demonic oppression can lead to depression, sickness, or other negative influences. *Many call exorcisms, exercising demons. If you have a fat demon, exercise it. Sorry, that joke was intended to lighten up after a serious subject.*

The Christian's Response

Clearly, make sure you are a Christian so that you can't be possessed (*see Soteriology*). Call for the elders of the church if you, or someone you love is possessed or oppressed (**James 5:13-20**). Know that God in us is greater than Satan, his demons, or any other problem (**Luk. 10:17; 1Jn. 4:4**). Be sober and watch (**1Pe. 5:8-9**). Don't be ignorant of Satan's crafty devices (**2Co. 2:11**). Resist Satan, and don't allow evil footholds in your life and mind (**Jam. 4:7; Eph. 4:27**). There is no temptation where God doesn't provide an escape—take it when He gives it (**2Co. 10:13**). Follow Jesus' example and use the spiritual power of prayer and God's Word (**Luk. 4:1-14**). Overcome evil through the name, testimony, and blood of Jesus (**Acts 16:18; Rev. 12:11**). "Finally, my brethren, be strong in the Lord, and in the power of his might. Put on the whole armor of God that ye may be able to stand against the wiles of the devil" (**Eph. 6:10f**).

Christ's parenthetical, mysterious Church; unified as His Body and Bride; our Head was dead, but now is forever alive.

Introduction

Ecclesiology comes from the Greek stems *"ekklesia"*, meaning Church or called out ones, and *"logos"*, meaning a word about, the science, or study of; thus **Ecclesiology is the study of the Church**. A key verse is **Heb. 10:25**, "Not forsaking the assembling of ourselves together, as the manner of some *is*; but exhorting *one another*: and so much the more, as ye see the day approaching."

Universal Church

The universal or invisible Church is comprised of all believers in Christ since the Day of Pentecost. There is only one universal Church (**Mat. 16:18; Eph. 1:22-23; 3:10; 5:23-32; Heb. 12:22-23**). The membership requirement is to believe in Jesus Christ as **Savior** to be members of this body. The main names given to this universal Church are: mystery (**Eph. 3:3, 4, 9; 5:32**), body of Christ where Christ is the head (**1Co. 12; Eph. 1:22-23; 5:30; Col. 1:18, 22, 24; 2:19**), a holy building, house, temple, habitation, or dwelling place for God's Spirit—metaphorically a holy place or home for Holy Spirit led activities (**1Co. 3:9-17; Eph. 2:19-22; 1Ti. 3:15; Heb. 3:6; 1Pe. 2:4-8; cf. 1Co. 6:19-20; Rev. 21:3**), "House of Prayer" (**Mat. 21:13 ; Mar. 11:17; Luk. 19:46**), and the bride of Christ (**Joh. 3:29; 2Co. 11:2; cf. Eph. 5:22-29; Rev. 19:7; 22:17**).

Local Church

The local or visible Church is a specific gathering of believers in Christ (organized with Biblically designed leadership) for the intent or purpose of meeting as a Church. Some definitions (see Merriam-Webster) also include: building, public, worship, denomination, clergy, and congregation in their definition. *I don't include them for these reasons: "building", because some Churches meet outside; "public", as some meet privately due to illegality, persecution, etc.; "worship", as that is only one of the many activities and goals* (prayer, Bible study, fellowship, evangelism, offering, invocations, ordinances, sharing, Bible memory, preaching, teaching, singing, music, etc.); "clergy" is included in leadership (but not called out as many use a variety of names for their leaders—minister, priest, pastor, preacher, brother…); "denomination", as it is just a way to divide, name, or describe the type of Church; and "congregation" is included by "gathering of believers" and are also called many things (lay-people, members, parishioner). A local Church could still exist with false leaders or ones the Bible disqualifies, but as **Rev. 2:5** indicates God will remove them; subsequently, they may be considered false churches. Included here "for the intent of purpose of meeting as a Church" to distinguish from just a group of believers hanging out, which might be called a fellowship, game, event, social, maybe even a Bible Study, but not Church, and not including the Church's purpose, ordinances, functions, etc. Hence, I do not consider two or more believers having a Bible study, or even Sunday School, Life Groups, or other Church activities and functions a Church or Church Service (which eliminates some ordinances and requirements), although Christ has wonderfully promised to be there *(Mat. 18:20)*. Most information on the local Church is found in the first verses of the Epistles and several recorded practices in Acts, as opposed to precept or command. Numerous local Churches exist around the world.

Membership and Attendance

The local Church membership requirement is to **believe in Jesus Christ as Savior and follow Christ**'s teachings in the Bible or what many call committing to serve Christ as **Lord** of their life (**1Co. 5:11; 10:21; Jam. 2:1-5**; cf. **Mat. 18:15-18**). Many local Churches establish their own individual requirements (e.g. new member classes, knowledge/service tests/catechisms, water baptism…to be a member in that local Body). Christians are commanded to attend church, but shouldn't have to be (**Heb. 10:25**). God does not specify how many times a Christian is required to attend Church, but most local Churches set their own attendance expectations based on desires, facilities, or needs. Many Churches have a multiple days a week with additional services or special activities (including Bible

Studies, schools, weddings, funerals, commencements, etc.). Churches that add works for eternal salvation (not just for Church membership), often refer to those works as sacraments, not ordinances (*see Soteriology*).

Ordinances—Water Baptism

There are two ordinances or commands for the Church from Scripture. Obviously numerous requirements may exist in some Churches for individual members. The first Church ordinance is water baptism. **Mat. 28:19-20** says, "Go ye therefore, and teach all nations, baptizing them in the name of the Father, and of the Son, and of the Holy Ghost: Teaching them to observe all things whatsoever I have commanded you; and, lo, I am with you alway, even unto the end of the world. Amen." The command is to water baptize, God doesn't really prescribe how. Therefore, the Church should water baptize and teach those baptized to follow Christ's commands. Some Churches require water baptism to be eternally saved (*baptismal regeneration*) and others believe it is to picture what spiritually happened when they were saved. I am strongly convinced that a person should only be baptized (**who/when receive**) after they have been eternally saved, in obedience to God's command (*see Soteriology—Water Baptism and Pneumatology— Spirit's Involvement with Saved*). Many Churches baptize (**how**) by total immersion (as the best representation of what spiritually took place identifying with Christ's death, burial, and resurrection. This mode of baptism with water covering the entire body best fits the Greek "*baptizo*" - to dip under or fully submerge). Others pour or sprinkle water on those being baptized, due to a belief, or scarcity of water in some facilities. Some go (**where**) out to a lake or river, others have a pool, basin, bowl, etc., within the Church for water baptism. Some only permit (**who performs**) the pastor or priest to water baptize, others permit teachers, the person who led them to Christ, lay-people, family, or friends. Why do some Churches practice infant baptism? The view is tightly coupled with the "who" and "when" discussion of water baptism above. Some Churches practice infant water baptism believing it: 1) saves the infant (nowhere stated in Scripture), 2) sanctifies the infant (or sets apart, or places the infant in a more favorable position to receive salvation; nevertheless, the infant doesn't understand, or make any choice), and 3) others view this practice as a dedication ceremony of the parents, Church body and friends. This does confuse the water baptism as a picture of what happens in salvation. View three is most consistent with Scripture and Church practice. Many Churches have services called "baby dedications" or really "parent dedication" services to commit to rear the child in the Church and to lead the child to faith in Christ.

Ordinances—The Lord's Supper

The second and final of the ordinances Christ set forth is "the Lord's Supper" (**Mat. 26:19, 26-30; Mar. 14:22-26; Luk. 22:15-20; 1Co. 11:18, 20-30**). Some call it a love feast, holy communion, the sacrifice of the altar, the blessed sacrament, holy mass, the breaking of bread, the holy eucharist, etc. The eucharist comes from the Greek root, "thanksgiving." The Bible does say that Jesus gave thanks before this Lord's Supper and certainly it is a celebration; we are thankful for His sacrifice. **1Co. 11:23-25** says, the Lord Jesus ". . . took bread: and when He had given thanks, He brake it, and said, 'Take, eat: this is My body, which is broken for you: this do in remembrance of Me.' After the same manner also He took the cup, when He had supped, saying, 'This cup is the new testament in My blood: this do ye, as oft as ye drink it, in remembrance of Me. For as often as ye eat this bread, and drink this cup, ye do shew the Lord's death till He come.'"

Almost all Churches equate this supper with a special presence or fellowship with Christ and other Christians. Catholics believe in transubstantiation, the belief that the bread (wafer or cracker) and wine (or grape juice) actually become Jesus' body and blood in a special conference of grace. Lutherans believe in what many call consubstantiation, but what they prefer is the sacramental union, which really says that the bread and wine are united with Christ's body and blood. Most mainline denominations see this ordinance of the Church as really a remembrance or memorial service of fellowship with God and other Christians through Christ's body and blood sacrifice. When first instituted with Christ and His disciples as a "Passover" observance, the type of the familiar OT sacrificial Lamb's body and blood was now going to be fulfilled and represented in the NT by Jesus final sacrificial body and blood. *Jesus metaphorically equated the OT Passover bread and wine with His body and blood as symbols or representations, memorials of His actual body and blood.* Regardless of individual or Church views, the Lord's Supper is not to be taken lightly (actually taking Christ's sacrifice in vain) by being drunk (**1Co. 11:21; Eph. 5:18**), having unexamined and unconfessed sin (**1Co. 11:28-31**), or making a glutton of yourself at the Lord's Supper (**1Co. 11:34**). Some having done these things are now dead (**1Co. 11:30**).

How often (**frequency**) should a Church provide the Lord's Supper? The Bible doesn't specify, but it says, "This do ye, as oft as you drink it, in remembrance of me." (**1Co. 11:25**) Some Churches observe this ordinance every week, biweekly, monthly, quarterly, semiannually, and others annually. Some prefer less often in order to not lose its special meaning and/or to reduce cost, while also attempting to ensure all members are able to participate. Some prefer to celebrate this ordinance of the Church at night as a supper, and others prefer the day or time when most attend. The central command is for each person to remember and contemplate what a great sacrifice and price Jesus Christ freely gave.

Church Discipline

The Bible commands Church discipline as a solemn warning to reduce sin, to help hold Christians accountable, and to restore fellowship in, and with the Church as set forth in **Mat. 18:15-18**). Church discipline has a minimum of three steps that should be performed humbly and in prayer. (1) Go to the offending or sinning person alone, trying to restore them. If the erring one repents and is restored the additional steps are unnecessary. If the sinning person is unrepentant, then the additional steps must be taken. (2) Take one or two witnesses back and plead again. Perhaps, the person caught in their sins will have had a change of heart and will repent. This is the desired outcome. If restoration and repentance do not take place, then the final step is necessary. (3) Take the issue/person to the Church (if the person repents, a brother is restored, and this matter may be dropped. If not, Scripture admonishes believers to treat him as an unsaved person, and try to win him to Christ). Unrepentant Church members require the Biblically obedient Churches to remove that person from the Church membership roll. Many Christians are not spiritually mature enough (cf. **Gal. 6:1-5**) to obey Scripture, or do not care enough for their brothers and sisters to go through each of those three deliberate steps. This is a critical indictment upon a believer, but even more challenging is the fact that most Churches are unwilling to perform Church discipline for fear of litigation or other political or financial reasons. This failure in the Church is demonstrative of sin and hypocrisy in the Church with fewer blessings by God. The Bible says if Christians performed "self-judgment" (**1Co. 6:1-8**) we would be wiser and not shamed before a world that already wants to blame hypocritical Christians for their own sin and their rejection of God,

Mission or Purpose

The Church's mission or purpose is to glorify God by our relationship with Him. When we love God, we also love man (**Joh. 14:15; Mat. 22:36-40**). When we love God, we obey Him and love our fellow man. Some have said, "We need to make a great commotion about the Great Commission." **Mat. 28:19-20** says, "Go ye therefore, and teach all nations, baptizing them in the name of the Father, and of the Son, and of the Holy Ghost: Teaching them to observe all things whatsoever I have commanded you: and, lo, I am with you alway, *even* unto the end of the world. Amen." Two commands that create a renewing Church cycle: Evangelism (sharing the Gospel of how a person can have eternal life by trusting in Jesus Christ as Savior; *see Soteriology*) and Edification (building up or teaching other believers how to mature and grow; **Eph. 4:16**). Edification includes personal and corporate (within the Church Body) Bible study, memory, meditation, prayer, accountability, service, praise, worship, fellowship, etc.

Spiritual Gifts

The Church has (through its members) received spiritual power and gifts through the Holy Spirit (**Acts 1:8**; **Rom. 12**; **1Co. 12**; **Eph. 4**; **1Pe. 4**) *{See Pneumatology for more detail}*. The Spirit enables the Church to overcome sin, Satan, death, and even the gates of Hell (**Mat. 16:18**) by His spiritual power, armor, and gifts to every true member in Christ's body.

Governance

The Bible doesn't specify many requirements in the governing or organizational structure of all the Churches. There are groups that consider each local Church independent, or autonomous. They may be on their own completely, or part of a larger group or main denomination (Southern Baptist, Presbyterian, Pentecostal, Methodist, Lutheran, etc.), which still may join together cooperatively for missions, Bible Colleges, seminaries, funding, additional Church planting, and key collaborations on major doctrines and statements of faith. These conventions or assemblies frequently include presidents, vice presidents, chairmen, and other offices. However, other than a statement of faith, each individual Church is independently governed and wholly autonomous. There are various permutations of polity within many coalitions of local Churches. **Denominations** are the group of Churches that at least share a common core of beliefs or statement of faith, and perhaps with some a common organizational structure. The other main type of organization is hierarchical or those with a specific governing body organized to direct all the local Churches under their ranks (e.g. Catholics, who have a Pope, Cardinals, Archbishops, Bishops, and Priests). This normally includes appointments and elections of leadership, doctrinal direction, funding, etc. Many have various nomenclature used for similar concepts of conventions, boards, councils, conferences, committees, ordained clergy, group leaders, pastors, teachers, and their congregations.

The Bible clearly says that Jesus Christ is the Head (**Col. 1:18**) and the Chief Cornerstone, and the rest of the Christians are members of His Body (**Mat. 21:42**; **Mar. 12:10**; **Luk. 20:17**; **Acts 4:11**; **1Co. 11:3**; **Eph.**

2:20; 5:23; 1Pe. 2:6-7). Next, it describes the apostles, prophets, pastors / teachers, and all gifted members (**1Co. 12:28; Eph. 2:20**). Many call their leaders by different names, but primarily there is a senior leader or primary preacher/teacher. This senior pastor, priest, elder, shepherd is normally the principal speaker and normally maintains the greatest influence in the organization of the local congregation. Some Churches organize themselves for ease of the congregation. Some rotate this shepherd to guard having too much influence or attachment to one individual. Thus, some Churches are led by one leading elder, pastor or priest, and others are led by multiple elders / bishops / presbyteries, (called <u>elder led</u>). There are Churches that deem themselves <u>congregation led</u>, which means a committee or shepherd brings votes to the congregation for their 1st, 2nd, and approval, or rejection. Many members feel this is perfunctory, as Godly people have already decided what seems best, and the congregation really just has an opportunity to speak up, offer a dissenting voice, or in essence veto decisions or direction, which rarely occurs. Motions are usually unanimously approved in deference to their leaders' recommendation(s). <u>Committee led</u> Churches can operate in similar ways as their leaders normally select committee members or individual members may nominate or volunteer to be part of a committee for certain tasks (e.g., pastoral search committee, personnel, finance, building, benevolence, etc). Congregation or committee led Churches assert that Christ is the Head and every member is a vital part of the body; therefore, all members listen to that Head, led by the Spirit, and share in that leadership. Elder led Churches normally believe that the elder(s) is in that position and is recognized by all as spiritually mature, faithful to lead and follow Christ's calling and direction.

<u>Elder Requirements</u>
The office or Biblical position requirements for a pastor, priest, shepherd, bishop, or elder (**1Ti. 3:1-7; Php. 1:1; 1Ti. 1:7; 3:1-2; 5:17-19; Tit. 1:5; Acts 11:30; 14:23; 15:2-6; 22-23; 16:4; 20:17-18; Heb. 11:2; Jam. 5:14; 1Pe. 5:1; Rev. 4:4, 10; 5:5-14; 7:11-13; 11:16; 14:3; 19:4**) are primarily outlined in 1 Timothy 3:1-7. The Bible says that a Church elder must be "<u>blameless</u>" (not perfect, just above reproach),

"the husband of one wife" (most require this to be a married man; many interpret this to not be remarried; Catholics frequently require unmarried—married to Christ's Church), "vigilant" (wise and hardworking), "sober" (sound mind and self-controlled), "of good behavior" (orderly, with decorum), "given to hospitality" (hospitable, loves people), "apt to teach" (instructive) , "not given to wine" (doesn't drink much alcohol; some require no alcohol and use grape juice for the Lord's Supper), "no striker" (not contentious or quarrelsome), "not greedy" (for money), "patient" (appropriate, gentle), "not a brawler" (peaceable or peacemaker), "not covetous" (not wanting others things), "ruleth well his own house" (presides as spiritual leader over his own body and family), "having his children in subjection with all gravity" (has sincere submissive children, maintaining that if an elder can't rule even his own house, he can't exercise leadership over God's house), "not a novice" (not a new Christian, so while having power, not to be lifted up in pride), "must have a good report of them which are without (has a good testimony among the unchurched). A Biblical Church elder must possess eleven positive character qualities. Conversely, he must not possess six negative attributes. Regardless of which governance model a Church holds, often the Church elders lay hands on those persons in this office (**Acts 13:3; 1Ti. 4:14**) while being ordained or commissioned through a Church led ordination service. These clergy also frequently obtain special licenses to perform marriages, funerals, etc.

Deacon Requirements

The office or Biblical position requirements for a deacon (**Php. 1:1; 1Ti. 3:8-13**) are primarily described in **1 Timothy 3:8-13** and closely resemble those of an elder. The first appointment of deacons in the church was to ensure the required service was not "neglected" while shepherds devoted themselves to study and prayer. This service of elders was specifically, "to serve tables, to care for widows." (**Acts 6:1-6**) The Bible says that a deacon must be "grave" (honorable), "not double-tongued" (honest), "not given to much wine" (doesn't drink much alcohol), "not greedy" (not money hungry), "holding the mystery of the faith in a pure conscience" (strong believer with pure conscience), "first be proved blameless" (examined and found above reproach), "so must their wives be <u>grave</u>, <u>not slanderers</u>, <u>sober</u>, <u>faithful in all things</u>" (with four requirements for their wife or they should serve and maintain their orderly home before trying to do so in the Church), "<u>the husband of one wife</u>" (some require this to be a married man; many interpret this as to not be remarried), "<u>ruling their children and their own houses well</u>" (again, presides well over his own body and family with sincere submissive children). Deacons are special servants in the Church that are also frequently commissioned, nominated, or called into that office (**Acts 6:6**) to help with the administrative needs in the Church organization or living organism.

Commencement or Beginning

There are various views and theological positions concerning when the Church began, and these are frequently based on how the Church is defined. Biblically, the Church began in the NT. The words "Church" and "Churches" are found 137 times, all in the NT. It was future from Christ. Jesus says later in His ministry about the Church to come, "I **will** build my church" (**Mat. 16:18**). Christ provides teaching about it (**Joh. 13-17; Mat. 13; 18:15-18**). Christ prays for it (**Joh. 17**). The Church did not and could not exist before Christ's death, burial, and resurrection (**Acts 20:28; Col. 3:1-3**).

The Holy Spirit's changed ministry marks the beginning of the church (*see Pneumatology*). Jesus talked about the future Spirit baptism by the Holy Spirit (**Acts 1:5**). The Holy Spirit came on the Day of Pentecost (**Acts 2**). This is where the Church was first observed and called the Church (**Acts 2:41-47**). They remembered the promise (that had been fulfilled) that the Spirit would baptize them (cf. **Joh. 14:16, 17, 26** f). The Church is Christ's Body and the Holy Spirit "baptized them into one body" (**1Co. 12:12-13**). The Holy Spirit forms the Church by Spirit baptism. Christ left (ascended to the Father), and the Holy Spirit came to gift and empower His Church.

People of God (Israel versus Church Distinction)

All the people of God for all time have always been saved by faith in God and His promised provision of Christ's death, burial, and resurrection. In the Garden of Eden, after the Great Flood, before multiple languages were in place, etc., believers were not called Israelites or the Church. To understand the Church start, one must not confuse the literal promises of the nation of Israel (square feet of land, national salvation, Kingdom Rule/Millennial rest, etc.) with the spiritual promises of all believers for all times (including those to the Church). Briefly in the OT, Israel nationally looked forward to Christ's coming, payment for sin, and establishment of His Kingdom. The Church was a hidden mystery. The Spirit's ministry was temporary in the lives of OT saints. In the NT, the Church collectively looks back at Christ's coming, payment for sin (His death), and looks forward to the Rapture. The Church is a revealed mystery (primarily through Paul's writing). The Spirit in a permanent indwelling of believers distinguishes the NT Church Age. What was the mystery? The mystery was simply Jews and Gentiles brought together equally in the one Body of Christ (cf. **Eph. 3:4-9; Col. 1:26-27; Rom. 11:25; 16:26; Gal. 3:28**). Although the term "rapture" does not appear in the scriptures it is commonly referred to as the "snatching away," of the body of Christ when He returns (see Eschatology). The Church rapture was also a mystery in the OT (**1Co. 15:51**). For greater detail and interesting review, refer to Lewis Sperry Chafer's <u>Systematic Theology</u>, Vol. IV, pp. 47-53, where he lists 24 distinctions between Israel and the Church).

Saturday or Sunday Worship

Closely associated with Israel and the OT distinctions with the NT Church, is the question on which day(s) should the Church worship? *Incidentally, the Gospels (although they reveal some Church doctrine) are truly OT, or Jewish history (**Acts 2** begins the Church).* Prior to the Law (over 400 years after the nation of Israel began), believers didn't have a single day in which they worshipped, or a national or commanded gathering together of believers for a specific day of worship. Israel began worshipping on the Sabbath (Saturday, the last day of the week), once they were commanded to do so by the Law (**Exo. 20:8-11; Deu. 5:12-15**). God promised blessing if Israel observed the Sabbath, and cursing if they did not (**Jer. 17:24-27**). God's reasons for commanding the Sabbath to Israel were as follows:

God's creation work (**Exo. 20:11**—He worked six days and rested on the seventh) and because of God's deliverance work (**Deu. 5:15**—He mightily delivered Israel from servitude in Egypt to their promised land), the Sabbath was a sign to the nation of Israel and other nations to know that God set them apart from the nations (**Exo. 31:13-17; Eze. 20:12, 20**). This Sabbath worship and rest is to be a "perpetual covenant" with the nation of Israel with a death penalty for breaking that Law (**Exo. 31:14-16**). Many additional specific laws and regulations were added to insure the Sabbath was not broken, although Israel polluted and broke the Sabbath so often that God cited this as His reasons for Israel's past and future time in captivity and tribulation (**Neh. 13:18-22; Lam. 1:7; 2Ch. 31:14-21; Isa. 56:2-6**). Israel still worships on the Sabbath today. The Bible promises that Israel will worship on the Sabbath again in the Tribulation and the Millennium (**Dan. 9:24-27; Eze. 44:24; 45:17; 46:1-12**).

The Church began as a mystery, when the Jewish nation was temporarily set aside during this Church Age, where both Jew and Gentile became a part of a new people of God in the Church (**Rom. 11:25; 16:25; Eph. 3:3-11; 5:32; Col. 1:23-28**). The Jews worshipped on Saturday. Jesus rose from the dead on Sunday, the first day of the week (**Mar. 16:9; Luk. 24:1-7; Joh. 20:1f**). The Church historically began worshipping on Sunday (**Acts 20:7**). God told the Church to collect their giving on Sunday (**1Co. 16:1-2**). Churches today worship on many days, but primarily worship on Sunday, some on Saturday, and some on different days with shared facilities, work schedules, etc. The persecuted Church in various locations around the world often meets at undisclosed locations and at different times. Seventh Day Adventists and Catholics often worship on Saturday. Most Protestants worship on Sunday, as the Church has historically done. Some judge others if they don't follow the Jewish sign and command under the Law of worshipping and resting on Saturday. God says to not judge a person for the day they choose to rest and worship and that no day is clean or unclean by itself, but that each Christian should choose their day to please God (not others), and be persuaded in their own mind (**Rom. 14:4-14**). Although most believers do not follow the principle of corporate worship or rest every day, every day for a believer ought to be a day of restful hallowed worship.

The unknown future is now made known,
by the Spirit testifying of Jesus.

Introduction

Eschatology comes from the Greek stems *"Eschatos"*, meaning last, end, final, or farthest things, and *"logos"*, meaning a word about, the science of, or the study of; thus **Eschatology is the study of Final Events**. A key verse is **1 Th. 4:16-17** - "For the Lord himself shall descend from heaven with a shout, with the voice of the archangel, and with the trump of God: and the dead in Christ shall rise first; then we which are alive *and* remain shall be caught up together with them in the clouds, to meet the Lord in the air, and so shall we ever be with the Lord." **Rev. 19:10**b - "Worship God; for the testimony of Jesus is the spirit of prophecy." Prophecy includes all predicted events at the time of prediction, all prophesied events that are future. As time passes, many prophecies become fulfilled or pass; prophecy includes eschatology, which are the remaining or events that are still future. Twenty percent of the Bible is prophetic. One hundred percent of these prophecies have been, or will be fulfilled.

Key Past Prophetic / Historic Events (Sequential)

1. **Creation (Gen. 1-2)**—*Old Testament (OT) starts*
2. **Marriage/Family Instituted** by God between one man and one woman (**Gen. 2:24-25**)
3. **First Sin & Death (Gen. 3)**
4. **First Sacrifice** (Offering) given (**Gen. 4:3-4**) of man's; God offered first sacrifice (**Gen. 3**)
5. **Flood**—Noah (**Gen. 6-7**)
6. **Tower of Babel (Gen. 11)**
7. **Nation of Israel / Jews** started—Abraham (**Gen. 12**)
8. **First Priest** mentioned (mediator between God and man)— Melchizedek (**Gen. 14:18**)
9. **First Tithe** (Tenth) Given (**Gen. 14:20**)

10. **First Prophet** mentioned (heard and spoke God's Word, especially the unknown future; formerly called "seer", as saw the future revealed by God)—Abraham (**Gen. 20:7**)
11. **Twelve Tribes** of Israel/Jacob (**Gen. 35:18; 49:28**)
12. **First Passover (Exo. 12)**
13. **Law**—Moses (**Exo. 20; Deu. 5**)
14. Sacrifices Commanded/**Sacrificial System** started (**Exo. 20**)
15. **First Tabernacle**—Tent of animal skins and place to worship God (**Exo. 25**)
16. Tithes Commanded (**Lev. 27:29-30**)
17. **Priesthood/Levites** started—1st Aaron (**Exo. 28:1; 38:21**)
18. **Judges** started (deliverers of Israel from enemies)—1st **Othniel** (**Jdg. 2:16; 3:9**)
19. **Prophetic Office**—1st **Samuel**; although Abraham, Moses...prior (**1Sa. 3**)
20. **Kings** (single ruler passed down thru birth or battle in Israel)—1st **Saul (1/2 Kings)**
21. **First Temple** (Walled house and place of worship) of 5 Jewish Temples (**1Ki. 6:38**)
22. **Israel/Divided Split**—Northern ten tribes and Southern tribes of Judah and Benjamin (**1Ki. 12**)
23. **Assyrian Captivity**—722 BC Northern Kingdom Tribes (**2Ki. 17:6**)
24. **Babylonian Captivity**—586 BC Southern Kingdom Tribes (**2Ki. 24:14**)
25. **400 silent years** (After Malachi, before Matthew)—*OT Ends; Inter-Testament*
26. **Christ's Birth; First Advent** or **First Coming of Christ**; God taking on human flesh; First coming to earth as the God-Man; God Incarnate; see Christophany (**Mat. 1:18; Luk. 1:14**)—*NT begins*
27. **Christ's Death/Burial** (**Mat. 27:50-66; Mar. 15:37-47; Luk. 23:46-56; Joh. 19:30f**)
28. **Christ's Resurrection** (**Mar. 16:9; 1Co. 15:20**)
29. **Resurrection of some OT Saints** (**Mat. 27:52-53**)
30. **Christ's Ascension** (**Acts 1:9-11; Mar. 16:19; Luk. 24:51**)

31. **Day of Pentecost**—Holy Spirit Outpouring and Eternal Indwelling (**Acts 2**)
32. **Church Age**—"Age of Grace" - Although the church has always been under grace, it began in **Acts 2**
33. **Spiritual Gifts (Rom. 12; 1Co. 12-14; Eph. 4; 1Pe. 4)**

Select Remaining Eschatology Events (Fairly Sequential)
1. **Rapture; Resurrection of NT Saints (1Th. 4:16-18; 1Co. 15:51-52; Joh. 14:1-3; Rev. 3:10)**. Rapture refers to all Christians or the Church (including those resurrected from the grave and still living on earth) are caught up to meet Jesus Christ in the clouds before ascending to heaven. Rapture views (when Christ returns in the clouds as it relates to the Tribulation):

    (1) **Post-Tribulation** – At the end of (after) the 7-year Tribulation. This is the second most held view, but doesn't recognize the Tribulation as Israel's last 7 years, prior to Christ's Second Coming (**Dan. 9:27**), it is "a time of Jacobs trouble" (**Jer. 30:7**), not the Church's. The Church is missing in the Great Tribulation (**Rev. 6-19**) and said to be saved "from Tribulation" (**Rev. 3:10**).

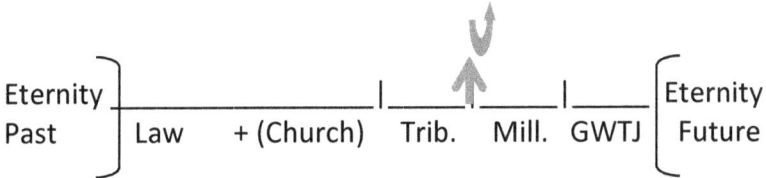

```
Eternity |_____|_____↑_____|_____ Eternity
Past  |  Law   + (Church)  Trib.  Mill.  GWTJ | Future
```

    (2) **Mid-Tribulation** – At the middle of (after 3 ½ years of) the Trib. The Bible doesn't show the Church or Christ on earth during the middle of the Tribulation, so few hold this view.

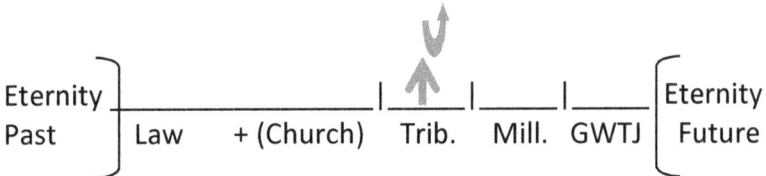

```
Eternity |_____|_↑_|_____|_____ Eternity
Past  |  Law   + (Church)  Trib.  Mill.  GWTJ | Future
```

(3) **Partial-Tribulation** – As believers mature (during) the Tribulation. The Bible never shows multiple comings of Christ and raptures, so few hold this view.

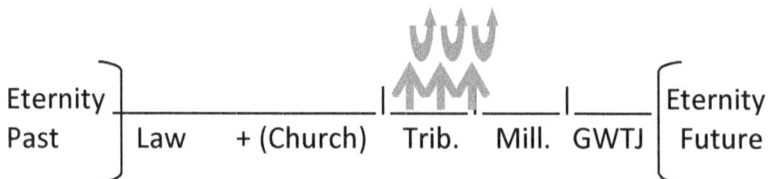

```
                              ʋʋʋ
Eternity |_____|ᴍ̂ᴍ̂ᴍ̂_____|_____ Eternity
Past     | Law   + (Church)  Trib.  Mill.  GWTJ | Future
```

(4) **Pre-Tribulation** - At the start of (prior to) the Tribulation. This view best fits a literal nature and purpose of Tribulation (Israel's cleansing), best fits the removal of the "restrainer" (**2Th. 2**) as the Holy Spirit indwelling Church, and most closely aligns with the book of Revelation's removal of the Church during Tribulation description. This is most consistent with the Jewish nature of the Tribulation described (e.g. 144,000 Jews from 12 Tribes (**Rev. 7**) and the two distinct witnesses like Moses and Elijah (**Rev. 11**)), and is most consistent with the many events that must happen after the Rapture of the Bride of Christ and His Second Coming. It also beautifully pictures the Church activities taking place in heaven (Marriage of the Lamb awards, etc.).

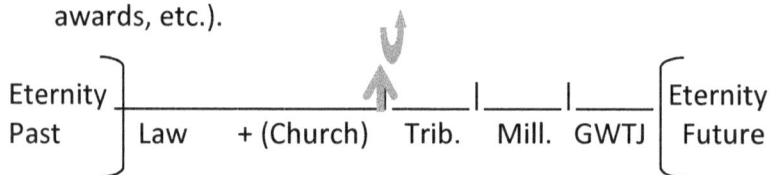

```
                           ʋ
Eternity |_____↑_____|_____|_____ Eternity
Past     | Law   + (Church)  Trib.  Mill.  GWTJ | Future
```

2. **Restrainer Removed (2Th. 2:7)**
3. **Judgment Seat of Christ (1Co. 3:12-15; 2Co. 5:10)**
4. **Worship in heaven (Rev. 4; 5)**
5. **Israel returns** to their Land—10 Kings Rule (**Dan. 7:24**)
6. **Temple rebuilt (Eze. 40-48)**
7. Judgment Restrained—False Security (**Rev. 7:1-3**)
8. **The Day of the Lord begins**—Daniel's 70th Week or 7-year Tribulation Period (**1Th. 5:12; Rev. 6:17**)

9. First 3 ½ Years of **Tribulation**--7 Seals, perhaps the false Babylon Church (**Rev. 6**)
10. **Anti-Christ** peacefully establishes Covenant with Israel (**Dan. 9:27; Rev. 6:1-2**)
11. Anti-Christ promoted by the "false" prophet (**Rev. 13:11-18**)
12. Man of Sin (lawlessness) Revealed (**2Th. 2:3-10**)
13. **144,000 witnesses** Sealed—12,000 from each Tribe of Israel (**Rev. 7:3-8**)
14. **2 witnesses begin**, like Moses and Elijah for the last 3 ½ years (**Rev. 11:3-6; Mal. 4:5-6**)
15. **Mark of the Beast (Rev. 13:16-18)**
16. Anti-Christ **destroys one-world false church** (**Rev. 17:16-18**)
17. **Two witnesses murdered & resurrected (Rev. 11:7-12)**
18. Silence in heaven (**Rev. 8:1**)
19. Marriage of the Lamb (**Rev. 19:5-9**)
20. Marriage Supper (**Rev. 19:9**)
21. Second 3 ½ Years **Great Tribulation**—political/economical Babylon (**Rev. 17-18**)
22. Seven Trumpets (**Rev. 8-9, 11**)
23. Seven Bowls (**Rev. 16**)
24. Satan cast down (**Rev. 12:2-17**)
25. **Antichrist breaks Covenant** (**Dan. 9:27**) at middle of Tribulation
26. Jerusalem overrun (**Luk. 21:24; Rev. 11:1-2**)
27. 144,000 martyred (**Rev. 14:1-5**)
28. Gog and Magog destroyed (**Eze. 38-39**)
29. Babylon destroyed (**Rev. 18**)
30. Jerusalem ravaged (**Zec. 14:1-5**)
31. **Second Advent—Second Coming of Christ** (**Rev. 19:11-16; Mat. 24:27-31**). Second Coming is defined as Christ Jesus coming to earth the second time (after the Tribulation) with Christians or the church. Second Coming views (when Christ returns to earth related to the Millennium):
    (1) **Post-Millennial**: At the end of (after) the 1,000-year Millennium. After the World Wars, most abandoned a Post-Millennial position as it was almost impossible to see "peace like a river" for the world and Israel as described in hundreds of verses (**Isa. 11:6; 65:19-25; 66:25; 66:12, 23,**

etc.) where animals don't eat meat, people live hundreds of years, and all the nations come to Jerusalem to worship the LORD).

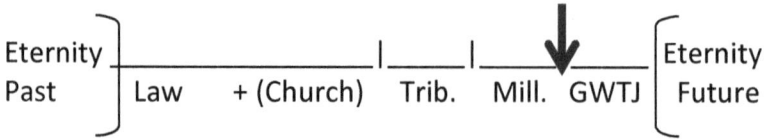

```
Eternity ┐_____|____|___↓___┌ Eternity
Past     │ Law   + (Church)  Trib.  Mill.  GWTJ │ Future
         ┘                                      └
```

(2) **Amillennial**: Only a spiritual (in it now), or no literal Millennium. There are hundreds of specific promises to the nation of Israel that can only be fulfilled by them, not spiritually in the Church (e.g. inches of their land restored, temple worship (**Eze. 40-48**), eternal rest/peace, earthly Kingdom reign of Christ).

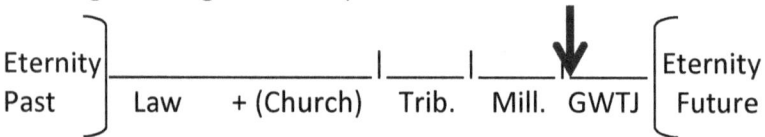

```
Eternity ┐_____|____|___↓___┌ Eternity
Past     │ Law   + (Church)  Trib.  Mill.  GWTJ │ Future
         ┘                                      └
```

(3) **Pre-Millennial**: At the start of (Prior to) the 1,000-year Millennium. A literal interpretation of Scripture and a distinction between Israel and the Church requires a Pre-millennial Second Coming. **Rev. 20:2-7** states six times in six verses that this is 1,000 years and Satan will "deceive the nations no more." Satan, certainly, is still deceiving the **nations.**

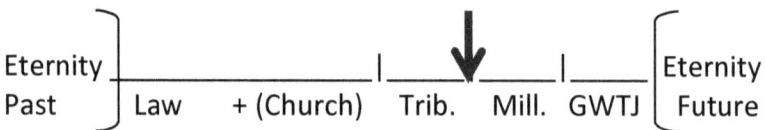

```
Eternity ┐_____|__↓__|____┌ Eternity
Past     │ Law   + (Church)  Trib.  Mill.  GWTJ │ Future
         ┘                                      └
```

32. **Armageddon (Rev. 19:11-19)**
33. **75 Days (Dan. 12:12)**
34. Beast and false prophet judged (**Rev. 19:20**)
35. Wicked remnant destroyed (**Rev. 19:21**)
36. **Satan bound (Rev. 20)**
37. Resurrection of OT saints (**Dan. 12:1-3**)

38. Resurrection of Tribulation saints (**Rev. 20:4-6**)
39. Israel judged (**Eze. 20:33-38; Mat. 25:1-30**)
40. Gentiles judged (**Mat. 25:31-46; Joel 3:1-2**)
41. Holy Spirit poured out (**Joel 2:28-29**)
42. Israel converted (**Rom. 11:26-27**)
43. **Millennial reign** of Christ (**Rev. 20; Dan. 2:34-35; 7:13-14**)
44. **Millennial Temple** (**Eze. 40-48**)
45. **Satan is loosed**, deceives and gathers nations (**Rev. 20:2, 7, 8**)
46. Gog and Magog destroyed (**Rev. 20:8; Eze. 38-39**)
47. Jerusalem surrounded and fire falls from heaven destroying the wicked (**Rev. 20:9**)
48. Resurrection of the wicked (**Rev. 20:9**)
49. Satan judged (**Rev. 20:10**)
50. Great White Throne Judgment **casts wicked into Hell** (**Rev. 20:11-15**)
51. Believers judge angels (**1Co. 6:3**)
52. Believers live eternally with Christ in Heaven (**Rev. 21:1-6**)

Approximate Timeline of Key Events by Number
(Underlined = past prophetic, fulfilled, or historical)

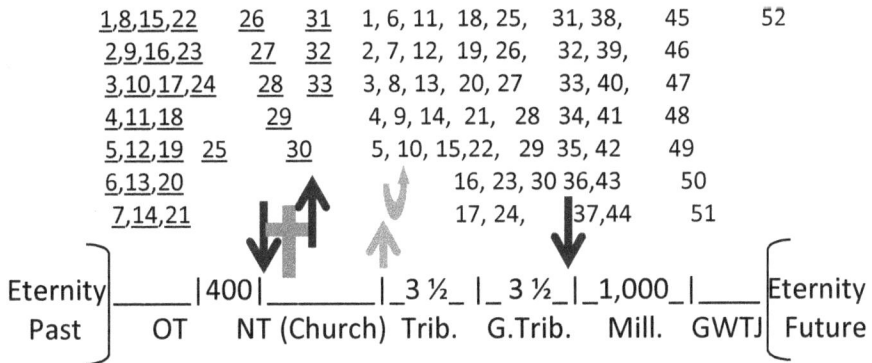

1,8,15,22	26	31	1, 6, 11,	18, 25,	31, 38,	45	52
2,9,16,23	27	32	2, 7, 12,	19, 26,	32, 39,	46	
3,10,17,24	28	33	3, 8, 13,	20, 27	33, 40,	47	
4,11,18		29	4, 9, 14,	21, 28	34, 41	48	
5,12,19	25	30	5, 10, 15,22	29	35, 42	49	
6,13,20				16, 23, 30	36,43	50	
7,14,21				17, 24,	37,44	51	

Eternity |_____|400|_____|_3 ½_ |_ 3 ½_|_1,000_|_____| Eternity
Past | OT | NT (Church) Trib. | G.Trib. | Mill. | GWTJ | Future

Bible Book Abbreviations
Referenced as **Book Chapter:Verse** (e.g. **Joh. 3:16**)
"**;**" shows same book (e.g. **Joh. 3:16; 6:47**)
All standard 3 letters, except 3 exceptions in *Italics*

OT Bible Book	Abr.			Abr.
Genesis	**Gen.**		Nahum	**Nah.**
Exodus	**Exo.**		Habakkuk	**Hab.**
Leviticus	**Lev.**		Zephaniah	**Zep.**
Numbers	**Num.**		Haggai	**Hag.**
Deuteronomy	**Deu.**		Zechariah	**Zec.**
Joshua	**Jos.**		Malachi	**Mal.**
Judges	*Jdg.*		NT Bible Book	Abr.
Ruth	**Rut.**		Matthew	**Mat.**
1 Samuel	**1Sa.**		Mark	**Mar.**
2 Samuel	**2Sa.**		Luke	**Luk.**
1 Kings	**1Ki.**		John	**Joh.**
2 Kings	**2Ki.**		Acts	**Act.**
1 Chronicles	**1Ch.**		Romans	**Rom.**
2 Chronicles	**2Ch.**		1 Corinthians	**1Co.**
Ezra	**Ezr.**		2 Corinthians	**2Co.**
Nehemiah	**Neh.**		Galatians	**Gal.**
Esther	**Est.**		Ephesians	**Eph.**
Job	**Job.**		Philippians	*Php.*
Psalms	**Psa.**		Colossians	**Col.**
Proverbs	**Pro.**		1 Thessalonians	**1Th.**
Ecclesiastes	**Ecc.**		2 Thessalonians	**2Th.**
Song of Solomon	**Son.**		1 Timothy	**1Ti.**
Isaiah	**Isa.**		2 Timothy	**2Ti.**
Jeremiah	**Jer.**		Titus	**Tit.**
Lamentations	**Lam.**		Philemon	*Phm.*
Ezekiel	**Eze.**		Hebrews	**Heb.**
Daniel	**Dan.**		James	**Jam.**
Hosea	**Hos.**		1 Peter	**1Pe**
Joel	**Joe.**		2 Peter	**2Pe.**
Amos	**Amo.**		1 John	**1Jo.**
Obadiah	**Obo.**		2 John	**2Jo.**
Jonah	**Jon.**		3 John	**3Jo.**
Micah	Mic.		Jude	**Jud.**
			Revelation	Rev.

Select Key Bible References

#	Study	Definition	Select Scripture
1	Bibliology	The Holy Bible	2Ti. 2:15; 3:16-17; 2Pe. 1:19-21; Heb. 4:12
2	Theology Proper	God the Father	Gen. 1:1; Deu. 6:4-5
3	Christology	Jesus Christ	Joh. 1:1, 14; Col. 2:9
4	Pneumatology	The Holy Spirit	Eph. 5:18
5	Anthropology	Mankind	Gen. 1:26-27
6	Hamartiology	Sin	Rom. 3:23; 5:12; 6:23
7	Soteriology	Salvation	Joh. 3:16; Eph. 2:8-9
8	Angelology	Angels (Elect/Evil)	Heb. 1:14; Psa. 103:20
9	Ecclesiology	The Church	Heb. 10:25
10	Eschatology	Final Events	1Th. 4:16-17

Select Bibliography

Chafer, Lewis Sperry. Lewis Sperry Chafer Systematic Theology, Dallas Seminary Press, Dallas, TX, 1980; VOLS. I-VIII.

Chafer, Lewis Sperry; Walvoord, John F. Major Bible Themes, Zondervan Pub. House, Grand Rapids, MI, 1974.

Evans, William. The Great Doctrines of the Bible, Moody Press, Chicago, IL, 1974.

Cambron, Mark G. Bible Doctrines, Zondervan Pub. House, Grand Rapids, MI, 1976.

Benson, Clarence H. The Triune God, Evangelical teacher Training Assoc., Wheaton, IL, 1970.

Lightner, Robert P. The God of the Bible, Baker Book House, Grand Rapids, MI, 1973.

Walvoord, John F. Jesus Christ Our Lord, Moody Press, Chicago, IL, 1969.

Ryrie, Charles C. The Holy Spirit, Moody Press, Chicago, IL, 1965.

Dickason, C. Fred. Angels, Elect & Evil, Moody Press, Chicago, IL, 1975.

Erickson, Millard J. Contemporary Options in Eschatology, Baker Book House, Grand Rapids, MI, 1977.

Ryrie, Charles C. What You Should Know About The Rapture, Moody Press, Chicago, IL, 1981.

Pentecost, J. Dwight. Things To Come, Zondervan Pub. House, Grand Rapids, MI, 1958.

Notes:
Study Bibles often have good Bible Doctrine overviews.

Unless otherwise noted, all Biblical passages are quoted from the King James Version (KJV).

www.ingramcontent.com/pod-product-compliance
Lightning Source LLC
Chambersburg PA
CBHW060755050426
42449CB00008B/1418